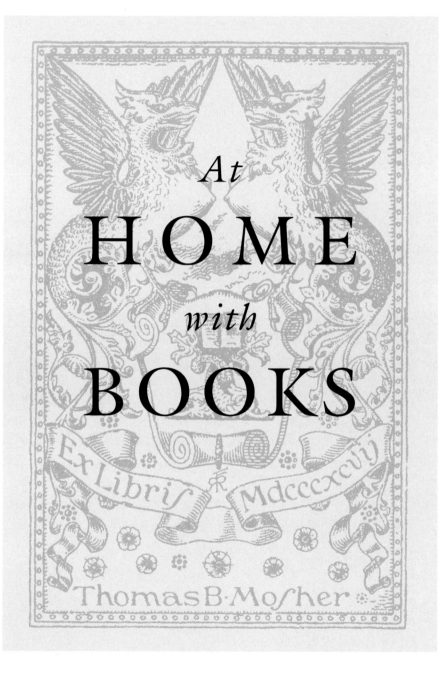

At
HOME
with
BOOKS

Ex Libris Mdcccxcvij

Thomas B· Mosher

At
HOME
with
BOOKS

How Booklovers

Live with and Care for

Their Libraries

ESTELLE ELLIS   CAROLINE SEEBOHM

CHRISTOPHER SIMON SYKES

Carol Southern Books
New York

frontispiece

ENGLISH INTERIOR DESIGNER NINA CAMPBELL USES "BIBLIOTHÈQUE"

WALLPAPER DESIGNED BY RICHARD NEAS FOR BRUNSCHWIG & FILS

(SEEN IN CLOSE UP ON PAGE 56) TO STRIKING EFFECT.

TO SAM, WHO WAS THE FIRST TO SAY YES. — E.E.

FOR SOPHIE AND HUGH, MY FAVORITE READERS. — C.S.

FOR KAREN. — C.S.S.

The authors gratefully acknowledge permission to reprint the following: Excerpt from "Artworks of Possession" by Jill Gerston. *Traditional Home.* November 1992. Excerpt from *Bibliomania,* a one-man show written and performed by Roger Rosenblatt and staged at the American Place Theatre in New York, 1994. Complete credits appear on page 247.

Text copyright © 1995 by Estelle Ellis and Caroline Seebohm
Photographs copyright © 1995 by Christopher Simon Sykes

Published by Carol Southern Books, a division of Clarkson N. Potter, Inc., 201 East 50th Street, New York, New York 10022. Member of the Crown Publishing Group.
Random House, Inc. New York, Toronto, London, Sydney, Auckland

CAROL SOUTHERN BOOKS and colophon are trademarks of Crown Publishers, Inc.

Manufactured in China

Design by Susan Carabetta

Library of Congress Cataloging-in-Publication Data
At home with books/by Estelle Ellis, Caroline Seebohm, and Christopher Simon Sykes.—1st ed.
Includes index.
1. Library architecture—United States. 2. Library architecture—Great Britain. 3. Private libraries—United States. 4. Private libraries—Great Britain. 5. Interior architecture—United States. 6. Interior architecture—Great Britain. I. Ellis, Estelle. II. Seebohm, Caroline III. Sykes, Christopher Simon. IV. Title.
Z679.2.U54S44 1995
027'.1'0973—dc20   94-42000   CIP
ISBN 0-517-59500-1
10 9 8 7 6 5 4

Acknowledgments

t all began in July of 1991, when two writers met and agreed that there was a gap on the bookshelf. A wonderful photographer came on board and interviews began almost immediately. The final results could have been achieved only by an extraordinary collaboration of booklovers everywhere.

Our thanks first must go to the people whose libraries appear in these pages. Their patience and generosity in allowing us into their homes have been invaluable. We are indebted to them, as well as to many others whose libraries are not pictured. Among them: Alex Alec-Smith, Grambs Miller Aronson, Diana Balmori, Glenn Bernbaum, Stephanie and Arthur Collins, Madison Cox, François de Menil, Rick Ellis, Cleo and James Fitch, Bernardo Fort-Brescia, Christopher Gibbs, Frank Giles, Charles Gross, Harriet Goodman, Shaun Gunson, Tiziana Hardy, Gerald and Camilla Harford, Eleanor Lambert, Anthony and Annabel Macall, Stanley Marcus, Linn Cary Mehta, Joseph Mindell, Eudorah Moore, Jan Pahorny, Sarah Plimpton, Toby Carr Rafelson, Claire and Maurice Segal, Paul Simon, John Saumarez Smith, Laurinda Spear, Judith Stonehill, Jerry Wald.

We are grateful in addition, to the many experts whose knowledge and experience helped in the development of special sections and the Resource Directory. They include: Martin Antonetti and Kimball Higgs (The Grolier Club), Peter Barna (Pratt Institute), Natalie Bauman (Bauman Rare Books), Alfred Bush, Joseph Ceterski (Rensselaer Polytechnic Institute), John Cole (The Center for the Book/Library of Congress), Jerilyn Glenn Davis, Victoria Glendinning, Elaine Haas (TALAS), Robert Harding (Maggs Bros. Ltd.), Warren and Gregg Monsees (Putnam Rolling Ladder Co.), Dr. Charles E. Pierce, Jr., and Grace Lappin (The Pierpont Morgan Library), Andrew Schloss, Kurt Thometz (The Private Library), Louis Weinstein (Heritage Book Shop, Inc.), Wilton Hale Wiggins and Douglas Lee (Twelfth Night West). Others who helped us in putting together the book were Frederick Krantz, Robert Rosenkranz, and special effects consultant Thomas H. Wright.

Appreciation is also expressed for the donation of supplementary art and photography: Peter Aaron and Erica Stoller of Esto for photographs of the New York Public Library, Dan Chatman's illustrations from "Care for Books," Adelaide de Menil's *Portrait of a Book*, Helen Dalrymple and Michael Dersin for photographs of the Library of Congress, Robert Lautman for photographs of Jefferson's library at Monticello, Margo Mulholland for her collection of bookplate art. Blumenthal, boussac of france, Brunschwig & Fils, and Clarence House contributed the trompe l'oeil wallpaper and fabrics that illuminate several chapters. Otto L. Bettmann gave many of the quotes and illustrations that appeared in *The Delights of Reading*, a David R. Godine book produced for the Center of the Book at the Library of Congress. S. Emmering, Antiquarian Bookseller & Print Dealer, Amsterdam, the Netherlands, generously allowed us to reprint the amusing early illustrations of libraries and book people that enliven the text.

A dedicated support group saw this book through from proposal to completion. Among these, none was more committed than Publisher Carol Southern, whose sensitivity and clear-eyed view of the book kept us all on track. We were all totally dependent on Eliza Scott, the most dilligent of coordinators, and Alison Stateman, who gave us resourceful writing support. Susan Carabetta provided us with a stunning design; Mark McCauslin, Jane Treuhaft, and Joan Denman expertly shepherded the book through production.

We thank them all. ↝

Contents

Wall–to–Wall Books

Literary Lairs

Private Pleasures

INTRODUCTION

At Home with Books

HY DO WE FEEL SO PASSIONATE ABOUT BOOKS, AND WHY DO WE ACCUMULATE THEM IN A SEEMINGLY UNCONTROLLABLE FASHION THROUGHOUT OUR LIVES? OUR LIBRARIES EXPRESS SOMETHING MORE THAN LEARNING—THEY LINK US WITH THE PAST, PRESENT, AND FUTURE IN A WAY THAT IS PORTABLE, AFFORDABLE, AND AESTHETICALLY PLEASURABLE. AS BARBARA TUCHMAN WROTE, "WITHOUT BOOKS, HISTORY IS SILENT, LITERATURE DUMB, SCIENCE CRIPPLED, THOUGHT AND SPECULATION AT A STANDSTILL." EVEN THE INFORMATION REVOLUTION AND THE INVASION OF THE CD-ROM CANNOT DISPLACE THIS ALMOST GENETIC ATTACHMENT WE DISPLAY TOWARD BOOKS.

BOOKSHELVES UP A STAIRCASE, A CORRIDOR OF BOOKS JOINING TWO ROOMS, BOOK WALLS THAT PARTITION A ROOM, DEFINE ROOMS IN OPEN SPACE, A HOUSE OCCUPIED BY BOOKS FROM ENTRANCE HALL TO ATTIC DORMER, BOOKS HIDDEN BEHIND MIRRORED DOORS TO PRESERVE THE PRIVATE MEMORY AND creative privacy of a writer, books in the bathroom, books stacked on side tables awaiting disposition, piled on bedside tables where people read, propped up by pillows . . . like children, there is no end to the persistent, lovable, but sometimes intolerable presence of books.

The most famous home in America has housed families of booklovers. Bill and Hillary Clinton, for instance, read books of all sorts, from political science to thrillers. One of the first things they noticed about the White House was that it did not have enough bookshelves, and they knew that without their books, the White House would never feel like home.

Or take the case of university president Harold Shapiro, who moved from Michigan to assume the post as president of Princeton. Before the move, his wife called in a graduate student to help her catalog and box the hundreds of books

Librairie G. Desbois
Livres rares et curieux
Belles Reliures
7, Rue Laffitte, Paris.

they both owned. They decided to arrange the books by subject—economics, politics, social sciences, travel. "This worked well for us," she said. But later, many years after the move, they accumulated huge numbers of new books, the familiar occupational hazard of an academic. What was to be done with these books? "Ah," she said, laughing, "we had to start a new library in another room."

Who has not experienced this problem? What is the best way to store books? By alphabet, some assert. By subject matter, others argue. In boxes in the basement, say the overwhelmed. The visually conscious may even go to the extreme of arranging

by color of the book jacket. Vivian Shapiro thinks that her new library room turned out to be inspired, in that it isolated the most recently published books. Welcome to another category—chronology. And so booklovers continue to struggle with the never-ending journey of book owning, a struggle that is expressed in *At Home with Books,* where the recurrent question is how best to fit more books into less space, and equally important, how to cope with the feeling that while books are overtaking your life, you cannot live without them.

When reading was limited to an educated elite, what to do with one's books was not a challenge for the interior decorator. The first known library was a collection of tablets in Babylonia in the twenty-first century B.C. The Temple at Jerusalem had a sacred library, and the Greeks started private collections as well as public libraries for the works of their great dramatists. Most Christian libraries in medieval times were in monasteries, and in the fifteenth century the oldest European public library, in the Vatican, was created. The earliest university library was at the Sorbonne in Paris in 1257, and most of the other European university libraries were founded during the next two centuries.

As the people who read books multiplied and literacy became democratized, places to store and read books became part of the interior living environment. By the eighteenth century, it was de rigueur for any proper gentleman to have an elegantly designed library room set aside for his collection of gleaming leather-bound books, which, while he may not have read any of them, enhanced his image as a man of wit and sophistication. Books took on an economic value according to their rarity, and specialized publishers proliferated, creating a book-buying public with new and different interests, forming libraries reflecting the wider range of knowledge made accessible to them.

Thus yesterday's image of the library as an elitist place, a hushed, paneled room devoted to the solitary pursuit of study, is fast fading, along with the draperies we associate with period furnishings. The library has been liberated. Books are no longer confined to a single space or a just-for-reading study or work area. Book people want their books where they can get to them, which is everywhere—close by and accessible. They may be piled or arranged on tables, pyramided on chairs, within arm's reach of the bed, or concealed behind screens. Towering stacks of books may rise up off the floor, creating a "bookscape" environment for the contemporary reader.

Libraries, perhaps more than any other room in the house, express the personality of their owners. Just as the contents of a medicine cabinet can tell a person's life story with uncanny accuracy, so the books people read say as much about their tastes, interests, and

THE CIRCULATING LIBRARY.

preferences as a psychological profile. "You can read a person by the books he reads," says historian A. L. Rowse. "Churchill's library is eloquent of the man."

This book, then, shines a spotlight on this revealing room and shows how a place filled with books can outrage, delight, intrigue, and seduce according to the person who created it. *At Home with Books* is about those readers—and the very personal, diverse libraries created for the passion they share. They describe themselves as people who are addicted, obsessed, consumed with the need to buy more books, find more space for books. Books are central to their lives, define their interests, professions, and values, and their book-centered homes define them. In fact, to people for whom books are a priority, reading rooms and creative ideas for housing their volumes can turn any room in the house into a library. Without exception, the people we interviewed spoke of an early love for and exposure to books, the excitement of getting a first library card, and hours spent in the neighborhood library. Many recalled the book-filled homes of their parents and grandparents and books read aloud. One treasured the small wicker rocker in which she remembers reading the books of her childhood. Another recalled travel trips with her mother and the allowance she was given to "go buy books." They told us how they stored them, how they moved them from one home to another, how their book walls got built or assembled, what they did when their libraries had to be shared or divided, and how to integrate new books with old collections.

Some are serious collectors, searching out an early Gutenberg, an antique leather binding, a Shakespeare first folio. "We value beauty and we value associations," says author Robertson Davies, himself, like most collectors, possessor of too many books, "and I do not think we should be sneered at because we like our heroes to be appropriately dressed." There is also the collector who collects simply for pleasure, without rhyme or reason. This character, among whom Davies counts himself, "loves books not only for what they have to say to him— though that is his principal reason—but for their look, their feel, yes, and even their smell. . . . His affair with books is a cheerful, life-enhancing passion."

Then there are collectors who are simply readers, people who amass books to read and then keep them afterward, regarding them as treasures that continue to glow with the hidden magic of their art. That includes most of us. We keep the books we read as children for sentimental reasons and to pass them on to our own children. As we grow up, we collect adult books, those we love

The Bookseller.

and admire and wish to return to. We go to work and add work-related books. We marry, we divorce, we have families, we grow old, and along the way, we hang on to our books. When former *Time* chief Henry Grunwald married Louise Melhado, the library battle lines were drawn. "Combining Henry's and my books was like combining two armies," she said.

People continue to make a home for books because books make a home. Book-centered rooms are described as nurturing, a comfort zone, an escape hatch, a place to retreat to for tea and talk, thinking and reading, recapturing memories, regenerating spirit and ideas. We found this to be true in a one-room studio walled with books, in an open-ended loft where the library was described as the heart of the house, or in a landmark brownstone where books were piled up the stairs and overflowed onto every floor. It was as true for the scholar as for the housewife, for the writer as for the businessman. Readers all, sharing the same feeling—that their books expressed their sense of home. Perhaps the most poignant example of this is the exchange between architect Thaddeus Kumierski, who was designing a house to be raised from the ashes of the 1990 Oakland and Berkeley fire, and his client. Kumierski emphasized the need for bookcases to impart warmth and stability to the reconstructed interior. The client agreed, then suddenly remembered sadly, "But I have no books anymore."

That a book has so much power seems astonishing, if one considers the unremarkable, boxlike, handheld object within which all this power resides. Books inspire fear (why else would a group called the White Aryan Resistance deface books in some American bookstores?) but they also invite pleasure, as seen in Jennifer Muller's dance work *Thesaurus,* which celebrates the five hundred words listed under "to move" in Roget's indispensable compendium. Books can kill: A falling bookcase causes an avalanche of books to finish off weakhearted Leonard Bast when he returns to Howards End in E. M. Forster's eponymous novel.

Perhaps the most devastating example of the potency of books is shown in the systematic effort of Hitler and his Nazi party to eradicate "degenerate" books from his newly purified nation. While the "correct" books preached anti-Semitism and the glorious German race ("To the Germans alone/The air does belong,/So friend Jew,/Move along"), the rest were seized and destroyed in a ritualistic burning, accompanied by an incantatory chant such as: "Against the exaggeration of unconscious urges based on destructive analysis of the people. . . . /I commit to the flames the works of Sigmund Freud."

Today books are threatened from a new quarter.

Computer technology, offering the ability to retrieve information from an enormous variety of sources and to reproduce it on a screen via a disk, seems to indicate that learning from books will soon be the old-fashioned way. University presses and libraries alike see doom in the possibility of book publishing turning into a computerized factory of disks and CD-ROMs. The library as we know it may be obsolete, like the still or the larder, by the end of the century.

James H. Billington, director of the Library of Congress, valiantly defends his noble institution: "Libraries are starting places for the adventure of learning that can go on whatever one's vocation and location in life. Reading is an adventure like that of discovery itself. Libraries are our base camps," he declares. His predecessor, Daniel J. Boorstin, adds, "The proverbial convenience, accessibility, and individuality of the book are unrivaled now or by any new technology in sight." And even CD-ROM multimedia pioneers such as Michael Rogers of Newsweek Interactive concede that "for the pure power of ideas, there's nothing like text."

There's a practical argument, too. As author Frances FitzGerald succinctly puts it, "Unlike a book, you can't take a floppy disk to bed." We support her view, offering as evidence *At Home with Books,* which shows not only how passionate people are about their books, but that the embracing environment created by books extends—and sometimes transcends—the pleasure of reading them. ❧

Libraries of Serious Collectors

 HAVE SEEN MEN HAZARD THEIR FORTUNES, GO ON LONG JOURNEYS HALFWAY AROUND THE WORLD, FORGE FRIENDSHIPS, EVEN LIE, CHEAT, AND STEAL, ALL FOR THE GAIN OF A BOOK. ∾

—A.S.W. ROSENBACH

JOHN AND JANE STUBBS

SEYMOUR DURST

THE DUKE OF DEVONSHIRE

RUTH AND MARVIN SACKNER

VICTOR NIEDERHOFFER

PAUL GETTY

LOREN AND FRANCES ROTHSCHILD

MITCHELL WOLFSON, JR.

John and Jane Stubbs

"WE WERE SO FASCINATED BY BOOKS AND BOOK PEOPLE THAT

WE DECIDED TO MAKE THEM A TWENTY-FIVE-HOUR-A-DAY ACTIVITY."

Jane Stubbs, a dealer in old books, prints, and drawings with a New York shop, Stubbs Books & Prints, never remembers not being surrounded by books. Her earliest memory is of a passageway walled with books which she had to move through before entering the other rooms of her home. She describes the house she grew up in as a "repository for my mother's passion for books." Looking back, Jane recalls that her grandparents' home was equally rich in books. She concludes that both generations shaped her image of home as "more library than living place."

It is understandable then that the house she and her husband, John Stubbs, an architect, restored should secrete those areas of the home having to do with sleeping, eating, dressing, and entertaining. Floor-to-ceiling metal bookcases were painted black to obscure them and block vision of a galley kitchen and bathroom. The Stubbses' bed disappears within an elevated structure that is braced by books. A back wall of books doubles as a headboard, "convenient when you read in bed as much as we do," she says. Equally accessible, a border of books serves as a foot board and decorative parapet for the storage closet they built under their loft bed to harbor a treasury of art books, portfolios, and drawings.

On entry a mélange of old estate library furniture sets the scene. Book cradles, carousels, carrels, book wagons, and library ladders were collected zealously by the Stubbses to "help in the preservation and presentation of books." John's books on architecture and the allied arts that he uses for the course he teaches at Columbia University line the longest wall of the "gallery," the first of two rooms in which a venerable library table is centered.

Jane's books on Southern cooking and history fill another, along with the leather-bound volumes of fiction and poetry she inherited and her formidable

opposite

THE ART JANE HANGS OFF BOOK WALLS, POSITIONS ON EASELS,

OR LEAVES FREESTANDING ON TABLES, CHESTS, AND FLOORS IS A

BACKDROP FOR JOHN'S FAVORITE READING CHAIR.

collection of books on "the evolution of the table." "I'm fascinated by anything having to do with food, wine, cocktails especially, table settings, and vintage serving pieces," Jane says. Shelf space on a wall framing the opening to the "salon" is shared with what John refers to as their "joint stock." Their idiosyncratic interests are revealed by a section on Naples, another on Lady Hamilton, Stanford White, and Flaubert, still another on fireworks, photography, art, and history.

Evidence of life beyond books can be discerned by the art Jane hangs off book walls, positions on easels, or leaves freestanding on tables, chests, or the window-seat rim of a romantic Turkish reading corner. Their home is reminiscent of a nineteenth-century literary salon. Books are interspersed with the most eclectic of personal collections: Wedgwood basaltware,

American pottery, framed English needlepoint, Pompeiian urns. Still-life arrangements of elegant shoes, tapestry, and beaded evening bags and spillings of antique and modern jewelry intrude on a carpeted ledge of books treasured for their fine old bindings or collectible twentieth-century jacket covers.

The library table, centerpiece of the room, is crowded with archaeological fragments, glass prisms, classical Greek sculpture, a head of Frank Lloyd Wright, ceramic bowls of potpourri, and Jane's cherished twelve-volume *History of England*, owned by the first governor of Mississippi. A free-fall assemblage of vintage china, glassware, silver, and candelabra adds to the creative clutter. Surrounding chairs are pedestals for rolls of Oriental carpet, weathered fabrics, and a twenty-first-edition *Encyclopaedia Britannica*, prompting Jane to explain: "When we

CARPETED LEDGE HOLDS A SURREAL ASSEMBLAGE OF EVENING
HOES AND BAGS, BOOKS, AND ART, ANNOUNCING JANE'S INVOLVEMENT
N LITERARY SOCIAL ACTIVITIES.

ANE TAKES A BUSINESS CALL, SURROUNDED BY BOOKS AND PRINTS
HE SPECIALIZES IN. PUGS, EDWARD AND BORIS, BOOKEND HER DESK.

OLD ESTATE FURNITURE—LIBRARY TABLE, BOOK CRADLES, CAROUSELS,
CARRELS—SETS THE SCENE FOR THE STUBBSES' LITERARY "WAREHOUSE
OF BOOKS," IN REALITY A TURN-OF-THE-CENTURY SALON.

invite people over for dinner, surfaces have to be cleared. Our friends are intrigued. They know we're pack rats and that this is essentially a book house."

Both Jane and John grew up in antique-collecting families that they credit with his interest in ancient architecture and antiquity and her appreciation of old objects preserved in literature. "My mother passed on her love of words and books to me," John says. "Jane's family was the last of those Southern people whose entertainment derived from their libraries. I'll never forget going through Natchez, calling up Jane's mother, and her telling me: 'Come for breakfast and come over early.' I arrived and discovered her mother and stepfather had been up all night. The fire was still going in the fireplace. They had been reading Chesterton and were quoting endlessly from him."

Early on the Stubbses discovered they both shared a collector's mania for books. "We eventually got to the point where we were spending thousands of dollars on them, and it became alarming to our friends and families," Jane remembers. "All of our salaries were going into buying books every week and we started worrying ourselves."

"We filled our first small apartment to the rafters with books," John says. "When we ran out of shelf space we created pyramids of books in front of the stacks and used them as tables. We were so fascinated by books and book people that we decided to make it a twenty-five-hour-a-day activity, a decision that drove us to look for a place that would work for business as well as home."

Together the Stubbses transformed an erratically proportioned loft, trapezoidal in shape, into a unique environment for collecting, selling, and living with books. "It became an interior landmark," John says, "attracting serious collectors, people looking for books to give as special presents as well as those who just wanted to see the way this strange couple from Louisiana and Mississippi lived."

"We're ready to start all over again," Jane says. "We now own more than eight thousand books and it's time to move on. None of it is on computer, it's all in my head and since I'm the one who does most of the buying, I know we need to consolidate the books we have here with the hundreds we store in our climate-controlled basement, the cases we have in storage, and the overflow of books we're constantly sending to Stubbs Books & Prints uptown."

"The challenge," John explains, "is to plan a home for books that does more than accommodate them physically. Books should be arranged so they're accessible and provide the pleasure of their presence. There are lessons to be learned from eighteenth-century home libraries. Bookcases were built to heights reachable by footstool. Today, when we run bookcases up to the ceiling, ladders are needed and for many people it's inconvenient. It's equally impractical to arrange books so low that people have to bend down to reach them.

"When you have thousands of books as we do, the library stack system may not be appropriate for human habitation but it's efficient. Setting up walls or partitions in different shapes, heights, and locations may also work to break up stack monotony. We're also beginning to think about walls that move on casters or tracks or fold out as they do in the John Soane Museum in London." ❧

above

BOOKSTEPS LEAD THE WAY TO AN ELEVATED SLEEP RETREAT
FRAMED BY BOOKS AND CAMOUFLAGED BY A TROMPE L'OEIL FACADE
THAT SECRETES A CLOSET HARBORING ART BOOKS, PORTFOLIOS,
AND DRAWINGS.

overleaf

"MY SHOP IS MORE LIKE A HOME," JANE SAYS OF STUBBS BOOKS &
PRINTS, A FAVORITE SITE FOR BOOK-LAUNCHING PARTIES AND ART-
RELATED EXHIBITS AND A MAGNET FOR WRITERS AND ARTISTS.

above

THE HUB OF THE DURST LIBRARY IS HOUSED IN A FORMER BILLIARD

ROOM. ARCHES LINED WITH ANTIQUE MARBLEIZED ENDPAPERS

HOLD BOOKS ON EARLY NEW YORK HISTORY, ARCHITECTURE, AND

THE PEOPLE WHO "HAVE MADE IT HERE": WRITERS, BUILDERS,

POWER BROKERS, ARTISTS.

Seymour Durst

"I DON'T COLLECT BOOKS OUT OF NOSTALGIA,

BUT OUT OF A LOVE OF INFORMATION AND HISTORY."

A builder and bibliomane, Seymour Durst has for the past three decades assembled the most comprehensive private collection in existence devoted to New York City. "I don't collect books out of nostalgia," Durst clarifies, "but out of a love of information and history." Durst's drive to collect anything and everything on New York was kindled by a discovery he made in a Paris bookstore in the 1960s. "I saw a book on New York by a German photographer and thought, This must be a topic that interests a lot of people. Then and there I decided to develop a library devoted to New York starting with the books I had already acquired."

Old York Library is the result: a center of information containing an amalgam of books, newspapers, magazines, journals, maps, blueprints, and a unique archive of New York memorabilia. "There's nothing I have that the New York Public Library doesn't have," Durst confides, "but there's a difference; anything anyone would want to know about New York is centered here. It's in focus and easy to get at. It's all arranged by subject so you can go right to a section and find what you're looking for."

Now numbering more than twelve thousand volumes, Durst's Old York Library has transformed his five-story home. Living space has been sublimated to a research library that literally occupies his home from basement to dormer roof. Books fill all twenty rooms except for four reserved as private quarters shared by Durst and granddaughter Anita. Those waiting to be reshelved are stacked on the bottom step of several floors, anticipating the next stair climber.

Durst makes no effort to neaten up for visitors. In an atmosphere of unself-conscious disorder, he has created a haven for lost and found books, documents, and prized New York collectibles: guidebooks, tourist folders, posters, cartoons, and postcards celebrating the city and its landmark buildings.

Books on urban planning and housing, arranged by streets and boroughs, occupy one section of a book wall. Other shelves are devoted to Native American history and rare books on New York architecture and landscape, including an 1847 edition of Wade and Groom's *Panorama of the Hudson from New York*. A much-sought-after six-volume first edition *Iconography of New York* includes maps and views of the city before 1915. It shares shelf space with folios of photographic studies illustrating cityscape changes, from Fifth Avenue to Washington Square Park. A less lofty view of the city is preserved in Durst's collection of vintage police gazettes and books on crime, including two arresting titles, *Sins of*

above

RARE VOLUMES AND PHOTOGRAPHIC STUDIES DEVOTED TO NEW

YORK ARE CATALOGED IN A ROOM ADJOINING THE KITCHEN. BOOKS

HAVE EVEN WORKED THEIR WAY INTO PANTRY CABINETS.

New York and *New York Unexpurgated*, an amoral guide to the underworld of Manhattan. These are counterbalanced with books documenting the city's judicial history.

Each of the floors of the Durst library has been organized by topic and mapped as if the books were being indexed in a catalog. A room on one floor concentrates on books on finance and real estate. These include biographies of luminaries identified with the city's development and expansion. Children's books telling stories of New York can be found on the ground floor, while books about the city by twentieth-century writers such as Russell Baker, Theodore Dreiser, Pete Hamill, Gay Talese, and Cecil Beaton are grouped on the top floor. Close by is a room dedicated to the fourth estate. "Press room," Durst calls it and shows off newspapers that were published when New York was an eight-paper city and dealers hawked copies of the *New York American,* the *Morning Telegraph,* and the *New York Herald.*

Still another floor is devoted to the world of theater, film, and entertainment. Durst appropriately adopted the Jacuzzi room on the fourth floor for a collection of girlie posters salvaged when the Durst Corporation replaced sex shops and theaters on 42nd Street with office towers.

Durst amassed his books by scouting secondhand bookstores in Lower Manhattan and by going to book auctions. Catalogs from the Strand Bookstore and Swan Galleries remain two other book-finding sources. When Durst discovers a book that requires repair, he turns to Cuban bookbinder Eudaldo

Gienesta, whom he calls "irreplacable." (Gienesta's ancestors were bookbinders to Spain's royal family.)

Durst turned what could be an intimidating archive into a user-friendly one. Hand lettered signs define books in each section. Every book carries one of Durst's self-designed bookplates and an "ID" card which he slips between the covers along with book reviews to give readers a helpful synopsis of content. A duplicate index card is filed in a card catalog, a forerunner of the computerized system Durst is setting up. Durst also amuses booksellers when he buys several copies of a book, explaining, "It eliminates cross-referencing." ✌

The Duke of Devonshire

"I AM A MIXTURE OF TWO CULTURES—BOOKS AND HORSE RACING."

Andrew, eleventh duke of Devonshire, lives in one of the largest and finest of England's stately homes. Built for the first duke of Devonshire between 1687 and 1707, Chatsworth, in Derbyshire, is filled with art treasures, books, and furniture. One of the house's most famous public rooms is the library, which the sixth duke, a bibliophile, redesigned in 1815 as a working library rather than one for display. With the help of architect Sir Jeffrey Wyatville, this dazzlingly elegant room houses the priceless Chatsworth collection of books, drawings, and manuscripts.

But the eleventh duke also has his own library, a private reading room far from the hordes of awestruck tourists, where he spends a great deal of his time. For unlike some people's image of the British aristocracy as a hunting, shooting, philistine bunch of blue-bloods, the present duke is an intellectual at heart.

His mother was a Cecil, a family that has produced many of England's greatest writers and essayists, including the author Lord David Cecil, the duke's uncle, who read aloud often to his little nephew.

"When I inherited the title and moved into Chatsworth in 1950, there was a competent collection of politics and literature that belonged to my father. But I cleared them all out and began my own collection. What I set out to do was produce a library so wide-ranging that a person of reasonable education could stay here for two years and emerge quite happy.

"Thus I have politics, biography, letters, classical fiction, twentieth-century fiction, oddities, a complete set of the first edition of Churchill's memoirs, First and Second World War collections, Bloomsbury, and a complete run of *Horizon* (the literary magazine founded and edited by Cyril Connolly from 1940 to 1950). I have a shelf consisting of books by friends,

opposite

THE LIBRARY'S DECORATION IS BY THE CRACE FAMILY, WHO PAINTED CEILINGS AND WALLS AND DID RESTORATIONS, OFTEN OF THE MOST EXUBERANT NATURE. "SITTING HERE," SAYS THE DUKE, "I FEEL THE ROOM IS A MIXTURE BETWEEN AN ILLUSTRATED MANUSCRIPT AND A FRENCH RESTAURANT."

TWO POTTERY PLATES BY QUENTIN BELL AND A DRAWING OF
CHARLESTON (WHERE VIRGINIA WOOLF'S SISTER VANESSA BELL
LIVED) BY ANGELICA GARNETT ARE SUITABLY PLACED NEAR THE
DUKE'S BLOOMSBURY BOOKS.

above

THE DESK IS COVERED WITH MEMENTOS BELONGING TO THE FAMILY.
"AFTER MY FUNERAL," THE DUKE DECLARES, "ALL MY GRANDCHILDREN
CAN TAKE SOMETHING FROM HERE." AN EXCEPTION IS THE SMALL
BRONZE BUST OF THE SIXTH DUKE. "HE STAYS."

good, bad, or indifferent. I also have a Disasters
shelf. The Duke of Windsor, incidentally, spends one
year on the Disasters shelf and one on the Royal
Biographies shelf.

"I can't read myself now very well, as my eyes
have gone, but I hardly come out of this room. I can
still read newspapers. When distinguished visitors
come to stay I get them to tell me what is missing
from the library. I recently bought Heywood Hill
(the famous London bookshop) so it is no trouble
acquiring books.

"My favorite reading as a child was Kipling—
the *Just So Stories* and *Kim*. Also Percy F. Westerman,
and George A. Henty. I enjoyed fiction about the
Romans. I've never been particularly interested in
rare or first editions, but I like certain sets of volumes
such as the pocket edition of Henry James
(Macmillan's London edition published in the 1920s).

"I tailor my books to visitors. In their bedrooms
here at Chatsworth they might find the *Oxford Book
of Short Stories*, the *Oxford Book of English Verse*, and
the short stories of Saki and Henry James, and perhaps Simenon.

"I enjoy the company of writers and if I keep
pretty quiet I can hold my own. I once wrote a book
about horse racing. Its purpose was to show to non-
racing people that the sport wasn't so philistine as is
generally thought. In fact I am a mixture of two cultures—books and horse racing." ✧

below

A SPLENDID BOOK TABLE AT CHATSWORTH DISPLAYS SOME OF THE
LIBRARY'S FINE BINDINGS.

bottom

THESE FAUX BOOKS INSET IN A DOOR HAVE PUNNING TITLES, SUCH
AS *PLAYS NEVER ACTED* (TEN VOLUMES), *BEVERIDGE ON THE BEER ACT,
VANDAMM ON SWEARING, WOLF'S LIFE OF LAMB, KANT ON HYPOCRISY.*

above

THE NOBLE PROPORTIONS OF THE MAIN LIBRARY AT CHATSWORTH.

23

Ruth and Marvin Sackner

"YOU CAN'T WANT TO BE A COLLECTOR, YOU'RE BORN THAT WAY. DRIVEN."

There are only three collections like it in the world. One is in the Getty Museum in California, another is in the Stuttgart Museum in Germany. The third is in the home of Ruth and Marvin Sackner in Florida. Their home is a center for the viewing and study of a discrete area of collecting, concrete and visual poetry. As astounding as what the Sackner library and art gallery contains, is where it is. The Sackners' renowned collection is harbored in an unimposing 1930s modern house on one of the waterways that crisscross humid, hurricane-threatened Miami Beach.

Undaunted by a climate that is hostile to books, paper, and art, the Sackners adopted the role of resident curators, conservators, patrons, and proselytizers of an esoteric form of literary art. Described as "comprehensive and idiosyncratic," the Sackners' archive harbors thirty-five thousand volumes that celebrate "the book and the word" and twelve hundred twentieth-century artists' books and book-related art. Walls, floors, and every furniture surface from hallway to gallery, library loft to bedroom and adjoining study, are dominated by the Sackners' global collection of avant-garde word-image art.

The Sackners describe their compulsion for collecting as a "shared creative love." Ruth compares the process of collecting books and images to the act of raising children. "The nurturing and caring are the same—a lot of rewards and a few disappointments," she muses. "Though I never showed off my children the way I do my collection," which she does frequently when she opens her home for museum, art, and book tours, as well as to writers and scholars who request access to study the collection.

Marvin adds: "You can't want to be a collector, you're born that way. Driven. It requires a mixture of

opposite

A HALLWAY WALL IS COMPLETELY LINED WITH TOM PHILLIPS'S *A HUMUMENT*, A SEMINAL WORK INCORPORATING 300 PAGES FROM WILLIAM MALLOCK'S NOVEL *A HUMAN DOCUMENT*. AN ADJOINING ROOM FEATURES ICONOGRAPHIC DRAWINGS BY JOEL HUBAUT IN TRIBUTE TO THE TOWN IN WHICH HE LIVES.

overleaf

HOMAGE TO THE LETTER, THE WORD, AND THE ARTIST'S BOOK IS EVERYWHERE, FROM THE HALLWAY TO THE 21 X 28-FOOT GALLERY/LIBRARY AND EXHIBITION SPACE IN THE SACKNER HOME. ANN NOEL'S PAINTING "*i*" BANNERS THE BALCONY; ON THE TABLE IS DONALD LIPSKI'S *BUILDING STEAM #277;* AT RIGHT, JOHN FURNIVAL'S INK-DRAWN WOODEN PANEL SCREEN, *FIFTY-ONE TOWERS OF BABEL.*

RUTH AND MARVIN MODEL ASTRID FURNIVAL WORD/IMAGE SWEATERS, HIS INSPIRED BY BECKETT'S "BREATHE," HERS WITH THE WORDS "BE FRUITFUL AND MULTIPLY" KNITTED ON THE BACK. THE SHOE SCULPTURES AT THE TOP OF FERDINAND KRIWET'S *WALK-TALK* PLASTIC CARPET ARE FILLED WITH POEMS IN MEMORY OF WRITER BOB KAUFMAN, BY SAN FRANCISCO STREET POET JACK HIRSCHMAN.

BREATH

ego, philanthropy, intellectual curiosity, excitement for the quest, and a genetic mutation toward the act of collecting itself."

"Our books were bursting out of every room of the house," Ruth says. "A young Cuban architect, Eduardo Luaces, told us he could double our book space simply by slanting the roof line of our house to make space for a balcony. In the event of a storm warning or a flood, we could move our most fragile books, documents, and artwork there, fourteen feet above the gallery floor. When Hurricane Andrew struck a few years ago, we did just that. Fortunately, our house was undamaged, but we decided to take additional precautions. In addition to hurricane shutters, we've now installed a metal water barrier at the base of our floor-to-ceiling gallery window. It gives us another four feet of protection. We're also in the process of converting a closet in the center of the house, on the second floor, into a storm vault to further safeguard our archive. Year-round air-conditioning, a sophisticated security system, and specialty art insurance give us peace of mind."

Asked how they got started, the Sackners take turns reminiscing. "In the late 1960s and '70s we discovered an adventuresome group of writer-artists who did breakthrough work integrating text and images," Marvin explains. "They transformed the design of a page by arranging letters, words, and paragraphs to convey symbolic as well as literary meaning. Size, form, ink, space, paper, and binding were as important as the text itself. Outstanding among the artists we met was an Englishman, Tom Phillips, whose books and paintings we now have in depth. We framed 162 pages from a first edition of Tom's *A Humument* (Human Document), the art book we bought from him when we first met. They line the wall in the entry hall."

"There were other influences that can be traced to our awakening," Ruth says, "none more then Stéphane Mallarmé's poem 'Un Coup de Des,' (Throw of the Dice). Published in 1897, this seminal work is believed by scholars to have changed the structure of the printed page in modern times. A work of experimental typography, it was designed to demonstrate that language is endowed with a mystery of meaning that increases with the number of different directions in which each word can point. However, it was Emmett Williams's book on *Concrete Poetry* that ultimately helped us realize the relevance of the books we were collecting."

Professor Peter Schwenger, who traveled from Halifax, Nova Scotia, to do research in the Sackners' library, describes its pleasures. "Every morning the library table was piled high with books I had asked to see the night before. In the still, cool air of the room I would turn the pages of rare and often unique books. They filled the senses: the fragile postwar pages or creamy laid paper under my fingers; the crackle or sigh as the pages were turned. The books were pulsing with color or staccato with hiero-glyphics; sometimes I found an unexpected object incorporated into the page—latex gloves, alphabet soup, fake fur—*Pat the Bunny* for the avant-garde.

"Large canvases and other large works of art in the room kept me company, as well as the books on the shelves. Their variegated sizes, shapes, and colors gave an illusion of movement, breaking ranks occa-sionally to spill into art objects laid out on the shelves like bright toys. As I browsed happily, it became apparent that these crowded shelves were thoroughly

ordered. Marvin even knew where to find books shelved behind other books. Every book had a story beyond that of its words—the story of its acquisition, its savoring."

The Sackners enjoy receiving visitors and corre-sponding with artists and poets throughout the world. Their archives include correspondence with fifty artists that they collect in depth. In addition to Tom Phillips and former poet laureate of the United States William Jay Smith, there are letters from visual/verbal artists John Furnival, Susan Barron, Joel Hubaut, and Vittore Baroni. "The interconnect-edness of the collection is intensified by the give-and-take our archive and exhibits evoke," Ruth says. "We established the archive to fill a need for an interna-tional, historic perspective on this work, but it's also a major pleasure in our own lives. We like to be sur-rounded by it all every day. We enjoy it so much that we maintain the library ourselves. We're both cura-tors and caretakers of our collection. We do our own cataloging. We even pack our own pieces when they go on tour, using acid-free paper and bubble pack. It's essentially a mom-and-pop operation." ᴄⱭ

left

ARRANGED IN A GRID, THE SACKNERS' BOOK WALL SYSTEM IS MADE UP OF SHELVES THAT ARE ADJUSTABLE AND DEEP ENOUGH TO HOLD A DOUBLE ROW OF BOOKS. PERIODICALS AND JOURNALS CHRONICLING THE CONCRETE AND VISUAL POETRY MOVEMENT ARE ORGANIZED ALPHABETICALLY, AS ARE THE WORKS OF ARTISTS AND WRITERS. PROTECTIVE BOXES, ORDERED FROM LIGHT IMPRESSIONS AND TALAS IN NEW YORK, SAFEGUARD DOCUMENTS, CATALOGS, AND SOFTCOVER PUBLICATIONS.

ABBIE HOFFMAN'S BOOK TITLE, *STEAL THIS BOOK...BURN THIS BOOK...WORSHIP THIS BOOK*, IS ENGRAVED ON THE FAUX MARBLE SURFACE OF KENNETH GOLDSMITH'S WOOD SCULPTURE.

LUCAS SAMARIS'S PLAYFUL USE OF TYPOGRAPHY, COLORED TEXT, AND PAPER FOLDED WITH HIDDEN MESSAGES CREATES A BOOK WITHIN A BOOK.

THE GARDEN, A KNIT WALL HANGING BY ASTRID FURNIVAL, GIVES VISUAL EXPRESSION TO THE WORDS OF SEVENTEENTH-CENTURY POET ANDREW MARVELL.

IN THE 2,500-SQUARE-FOOT LIBRARY DESIGNED BY FRANCIS C. KLEIN,

A CENTRAL TABLE HOLDS BOOKS THAT MR. NIEDERHOFFER IS

CURRENTLY STUDYING, PLUS BOOKS TO BE RETURNED TO THE

STACKS. EVERY BOOK IS CATALOGED.

Victor Niederhoffer

Broker Victor Niederhoffer is perfectly comfortable in the volatile world of high finance. Yet he also inhabits the hushed, scholarly, reflective society of books, having over the years assembled in his huge house in Connecticut a library that many a bibliophile might envy. He lives there with his wife and six daughters. While the top floor hums with the instant-access computerized machinery connected to Wall Street, a large part of the ground and below-ground floors is committed to books.

Mr. Niederhoffer's story could have come from one of the nineteenth-century novels on his shelves. His father was a policeman with the Thirteenth Precinct on Manhattan's Lower East Side. "He loved books and read all the time. When he died five librarians came to his funeral. Publishers in the neighborhood got to know of his interest, and would give him books. In this way, he built up a remarkable library. I inherited his love for books, and his library was the beginning of mine."

His father was in debt all his life, but because of his scholarly interests his son had the advantage of whole worlds within reach. At Harvard, Niederhoffer wrote a Ph.D. thesis on newspapers and how they affect economic events. Through handling many old newspapers for his research, he realized that the power of the printed word derives not only from its content but also from its context. The size of type, the surrounding advertising, the blocking out of the pages, the feel of the paper, all contributed to his deeper understanding of the historical material.

It was this physicality of handling printed material that fired his interest in adding his own book collection to that of his father. "When you pick up a first edition you know this is how it felt when it first came out, and you feel its historical presence actually within your grasp." For Niederhoffer, this visceral connection with the book is a crucial part of the excitement he experiences from his library.

With the help of book dealers such as Natalie and David Bauman among others, Victor Niederhoffer now has roughly eighteen thousand books, with the widest range of subject matter imaginable—cities, sports, hobbies, biography, world history, war, piracy, frauds and counterfeiters, children's books, first editions, poetry and drama, early economics, biology, medicine, industry, heroism.

"I wanted," he says, "to create a library of the key achievements of Western civilization—the most influential movers and shakers—any individual who made a significant impact on Western culture, any person or action that made a difference to our world." With that understanding, Mr. Niederhoffer's library makes brilliant sense.

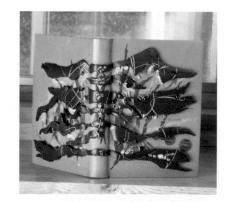

Besides the books, there are other items of great value here. A Nuremberg map dated 1493, for instance, a *Hamlet* first folio, letters from Washington and Jefferson, Edison's drawings of the first light-bulbs, papers leading up to the Declaration of Independence. Historical figures come to life through rare documents such as an eyewitness diary about Lincoln's assassination, Mussolini's leather-bound scrapbook, an oversize illustrated record of the coronation of Nicholas and Alexandra of Russia, unusual biographies of lowlifes and petty criminals (perhaps in recognition of his father's profession in law enforcement).

In spite of their quality, Mr. Niederhoffer firmly believes that his books are to be read, not gazed at respectfully on distant shelves. The library, designed by architect Francis C. Klein, invites browsing, with comfortable sofas, accessible shelves, good lighting, no locks, no closed doors. Indeed, his dealers feel that some of the materials are all too accessible.

Mr. Niederhoffer conceded to temperature control, and precautions such as keeping certain docu-ments under glass. But true to his belief in the power of the book as object, he likes to handle his books, to show them to people, to read aloud from the pages. This library is *used*. His family is thoroughly book minded. There is no TV, a medium Niederhoffer deplores as antagonistic to learning. Like his father before him, he routinely reads to his children at any time of day or night, and especially at mealtimes. There is a special children's section of his library for family get-togethers.

This informality belies the intense commitment of the collector to his passion. In the basement, a vast underground vault with deep pile carpeting and beautiful wood paneling, he keeps contemporary first editions and whole libraries he acquired from the homes of Ayn Rand and Maynard Keynes, among others. With restless energy, he roams his house, shoeless, tieless, in sweats, young children at his feet, the picture of a man at ease. Yet therein lies a paradox. For as he shows the visitor around, door after door opens to reveal the secrets of this man's heart—displays of antique children's toys, a museum of

far left

ANTIQUE BOOKENDS DEPICTING ELEPHANTS AND PALM TREES ARE WELL CHOSEN TO EMBRACE A COLLECTION OF BOOKS ON AFRICA.

left

A 1937 FIRST EDITION OF *THE HOBBIT* BY J.R.R. TOLKIEN, BOUND BY AMERICAN BOOKBINDER DONALD GLAISTER, STUDDED WITH EMERALDS, RUBIES, SAPPHIRES, OPALS, AND DIAMONDS.

silver salvers, chalices, and ornaments, rare board games, an assortment of mechanical musical instruments ("Want to hear one?" he asks, as the plunk-te-plunk of an automatic piano and drum starts grinding away). Look carefully, and behind the casual expression in his eyes one sees the glint of collecting mania.

And when he returns to the main library, he cannot conceal his satisfaction in what he has gathered here. He will take a book out, open it, explain its history and the source of its power, then return it to its shelf, all carried out with a kind of suppressed pleasure. The feeling is contagious. After exposure to several of these great volumes, one is left with the feeling that the sum of the best of human knowledge has truly been brought together in this masterfully conceived and executed library. "This place is not meant to be a repository or Baedeker of everything that's been written," he says. "I don't expect to satisfy everyone with a thirst for knowledge here. But I could spend a lifetime in this room and not be bored, and that's the purpose of this collection." 🖎

Paul Getty

"BOOKS, LIKE WINE, NEED TO BE KEPT AT A REGULAR,

UNFLUCTUATING TEMPERATURE."

Just as few churches today are built on the scale of the splendid Gothic cathedrals of the Christian world, so libraries built in the late twentieth century have little of the authority or grandeur of the great eighteenth-century ones. That is why Paul Getty's recently completed library in Oxfordshire, England, is so exhilarating. Not only is it modeled on the scale of some of the finest scholarly libraries dating back centuries, but it contains state-of-the-art technology for preserving its books for centuries to come.

Housed in a castlelike folly attached to Mr. Getty's main house, the library contains over five thousand rare books and manuscripts exemplifying the art of the book. There are fine examples of early printing on vellum, rare illustrated books and early medieval illuminated manuscripts, modern fine-press books with examples from William Morris's Kelmscott Press and the Ashendene Press, samples of Victorian color printing, and a collection of book bindings dating from medieval to modern times.

Director of this collection is Bryan Maggs, an antiquarian bookseller (of Maggs Bros., a family firm since 1853), who has guided Mr. Getty in his acquisitions for twenty years. "Mr. Getty had been collecting books for so long," explains Mr. Maggs, "that they outgrew his house in London. So this library has been in the works for quite some time. Although it is a private library, bibliographic societies and serious scholars may come here to examine the collections, and often the books are lent to exhibitions."

The first impression of the library is of light and perspective. The skylights, while letting in natural light, are treated to screen out ultraviolet rays. All other lights are on dimmers, designed to isolate the area where a scholar may be working. The wood used throughout the room is oak, reminiscent of a medieval library. A large fireplace gives the space warmth.

The air is thermostatically controlled, with humidifiers lending the right moisture (central heating is famously bad for books). "The cooler the better," says Mr. Maggs, leading the visitor down two levels

opposite

THE SPECTACULAR VAULTED CEILINGS, SKYLIGHTS, FINELY CARVED

BALUSTRADE, AND BOOKSHELVES GIVE THIS JUST-FINISHED LIBRARY

AN IMMEDIATE SENSE OF LONGEVITY.

above

PAUL GETTY CHOSE A CASTLE IN WHICH TO HOUSE HIS COLLECTION.

left

THE BOOKS, ARRANGED CHRONOLOGICALLY, ARE LOOKED AFTER LIKE ROYALTY ON BAIZE-LINED SHELVES, WITH SOFT LIGHTING AND ORNAMENTAL CARVING TO ENHANCE THEIR BEAUTY.

below the earth to the huge air-conditioning plant. Holes have been placed in the backs of the shelves to circulate cool air around the books while leaving the main body of the room warm enough for human comfort. "Books, like wine, need to be kept at a regular, unfluctuating temperature," explains Mr. Maggs.

The shelves are extra deep, for air circulation, and all adjustable. They are lined in billiard-table baize, so a book is not marked when removed. Pull-out shelves on rollers have been designed for large folio volumes. In case of fire—every librarian's greatest dread—sprinklers pour out Halon gas rather than water; a wet book is every librarian's other greatest dread. If by some terrible accident books *do* get wet, the best thing, according to Mr. Maggs, is to freeze them. This stabilizes them and prevents fungal growth before restoration. Naturally, there is a freezer in Mr. Getty's basement.

If pressed, Mr. Maggs will take the visitor into this basement where, along with the freezer, there is a vault containing the most valuable works in Mr. Getty's collection, which include the Ulm 1482 edition of Ptolemy's atlas, printed on vellum; a copy of the Kelmscott Press edition of Chaucer, also printed on vellum; and books belonging to Charles I and Elizabeth I. Mr. Maggs handles these books with reverence, because he knows the value of a book. He can pick up a volume and immediately tell you its date. "I grew up looking at and handling books. It's the only way to learn," he says. He tactfully declined, however, to put a figure on Mr. Getty's library. Booklovers do not discuss that kind of thing. ℘

top left

CAMPI PHLEGRAE, BOUND IN VELLUM BY EDWARDS OF HALIFAX, CIRCA 1776.

top center

KELMSCOTT PRESS EDITION OF CHAUCER BY WILLIAM MORRIS, 1894.

top right

KEATS POEM BOUND IN VELLUM BY SANGORSKI AND SUTCLIFFE, 1912–14.

above

A BIRD'S-EYE VIEW OF THE LIBRARY.

Loren and Frances Rothschild

"THE BOOK COLLECTOR MUST TAKE EXTRAORDINARY STEPS TO GAIN

THE PLEASURES SO EASILY AFFORDED THE ART COLLECTOR."

Book collecting takes various forms. Some collect the book for its quality as an object, that is, its fine binding, parchment, printing. Some collect books for their rarity value. Still others collect books because of their authors. Loren Rothschild is such a man, and his preeminent author is the great eighteenth-century poet, biographer, moralist, and lexicographer Samuel Johnson.

There are other Johnsonians around the world. With her late husband Donald Hyde, Viscountess Eccles built up perhaps the greatest collection of Johnson manuscripts, books, and letters ever assembled. Herman W. Liebert, Arthur A. Houghton, Jr., and Arthur G. Rippey are other passionate collectors of Johnsoniana. But Loren Rothschild, lone representative of this elite band on the West Coast of the United States, entered the lists almost fifteen years ago with his wife, Frances, and has assiduously accumulated Johnson material as it became available.

"In 1977 I was reading *Samuel Johnson,* the biography by W. Jackson Bate," explains Mr. Rothschild, "and I was struck by the greatness and humanity of Johnson. That's how I started."

A book collector since high school, Rothschild has over the years collected books and manuscripts of other eighteenth-century writers, including Oliver Goldsmith, Henry Fielding, and Alexander Pope. The nineteenth century is represented by Sir Richard Burton, and the twentieth by Somerset Maugham, Evelyn Waugh, and Paul Theroux, all writers he greatly admires.

An Anglophile, obviously, he wanted an English library to accommodate these treasures. Three years in the construction, his elegant wood-paneled room has indeed an English feel, with its fireplace, paintings, and comfortable seating. But we also sense the influence of California in the choice of the room's light pine wood, brightly colored furnishings, and the very un-English sun that beams in through the windows most of the year.

The main library adjoins a smaller anteroom called the Gallery, where secondary material is stored, and where scholars may study papers and documents made available to them on request by the owners.

opposite

THIS IS THE MOST FAMOUS PORTRAIT OF SAMUEL JOHNSON,
PAINTED BY SIR JOSHUA REYNOLDS IN 1775. REPRODUCED
EVERYWHERE, IT IS CALLED *BLINKING SAM.*

below left

RARE DUST JACKETS OF LOREN ROTHSCHILD'S COLLECTION OF
W. SOMSERSET MAUGHAM FIRST EDITIONS.

below right

IN THE GALLERY, AN ENGLISH TABLE DISPLAYING A SAMUEL JOHNSON
PORTRAIT IS USED BY VISITING SCHOLARS AND STUDENTS.

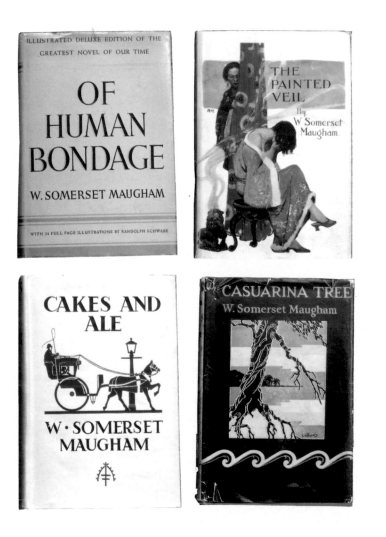

Asked if it is more exciting to possess manuscripts rather than printed books, Mr. Rothschild quotes Lady Eccles: "It's like blood compared to water."

But it is not easy being such a proud owner of these priceless documents. As Mr. Rothschild explained in the preface to the catalog of an exhibition of letters and books relating to Johnson that he organized in 1986: "A book collector misses the pleasure available to the art collector, whose prizes may be permanently displayed on the walls of his house for his own and his friends' appreciation. Books are usually small, externally uninteresting, and normally not very attractive. The spines on a shelf of Johnsoniana do not strike the eye of an observer with the impact of a wall of Impressionist paintings. The book collector must therefore take extraordinary steps to gain the pleasures so easily afforded the art collector."

As well as opening his library by invitation to a few aficionados, Mr. Rothschild also lends his material to universities, hoping to ignite the same enthusiasm in others. Meanwhile, he continues to buy when he can, making regular visits to London. Fortunately the library was planned to accommodate future acquisitions made by this dedicated collector. ✑

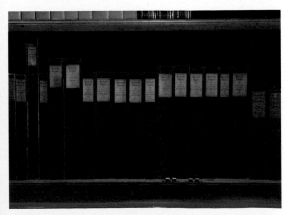

above

BEAUTIFULLY PANELED IN PINE, THIS LIBRARY HAS A CLASSICAL
LOOK, ENHANCED BY GLASSED-IN SHELVING AND CHINTZ
FURNISHINGS.

left

THE WORKS OF JAMES BOSWELL, JOHNSON'S LIVELY BIOGRAPHER.

Mitchell Wolfson, Jr.

"I AM A GATHERER, NOT A HOARDER. I PREFER TO FIND, NOT TO KEEP."

When I was in the cradle, I reached out for something. My mother said I was a born collector." Thus began Mitchell Wolfson Jr.'s career, culminating in the Wolfsonian Foundation, founded in 1986 for the study of European and American cultural history from 1885 to 1945, including a library filled with rare books and prints and periodicals of the period, currently being cataloged and preserved by curators. Based in Miami, Florida, and Genoa, Italy, the foundation is the brainchild of Mr. Wolfson, a Miami native whose intellectual interests are so wide-ranging that the dates he has chosen to represent his collections seem altogether too narrow. "I thought those sixty years between 1885 and 1945 were ushering in the New World Order," Mr. Wolfson explains, "but it wasn't the New World Order at all. I should have extended the period up to 1990, when the Berlin Wall came down. Now we are caught in the middle."

This dilemma is one of many facing this intellectual whirlwind of a man. Like his name, he wolfs down information on literature, art, music, and politics written in many languages (he speaks fluent French and Italian) as he races round the world finding objects for his collections. "I think for Mr. Wolfson, it's the process of collecting that is most important," says the foundation's librarian, Jim Findlay. "He really loves the process leading up to and including the buying of the book or object. Once it is acquired, it goes on a shelf and is admired from time to time. I think many collectors feel the same way. It's the hunt that really pleases them."

"Maybe a third of my books were inherited from my great-grandparents and grandparents. My mother's family came from Montgomery, Pensacola, and New Orleans, and my father's family came from Key West, so if you look at my library it's exactly what every politically correct Southern family would have."

His books also reflect his own eclectic interests, from trains (his own private railroad car, in which he traveled with friends all over the United States, was irreparably damaged by Hurricane Andrew) to vintage books, and from Christopher Columbus to Florida's flora, fauna, and history. Most important books go to his museum, housed in an extraordinary Mediterranean-style 1920s former storage company

top

RARE BOOKS, PORTFOLIOS, AND ARTWORK ARE DISPLAYED IN MITCHELL WOLFSON'S PRIVATE STUDY AT HOME.

above

SAMPLES OF THE WIDE-RANGING BOOK COLLECTIONS AT THE WOLFSONIAN FOUNDATION, INCLUDING GERMAN, ITALIAN, CUBAN, AND U.S. POLITICAL PUBLICATIONS.

building in Miami Beach. Others remain in his own house, within easy reach of this omnivorous reader.

"When I travel I take at least ten books with me. I approach a book as an icon and I read it as a ritual. It's almost a religious experience. I cannot read a book casually. I prepare the book before it gets read. I open it up from the center so as not to damage the spine, and then I always read with a pencil in hand so if I come to a passage that is particularly helpful to me I can make light notations that can be erased later."

Paradoxically, he lives in a place with little respect for books. Miami, with its hot and humid climate, is famously inhospitable to the preservation of books. "I like to defy nature," he declares, "and since books were never supposed to be in residence in tropical Florida, it's been a challenge for me to see how long they'll last. Nothing you'll see in anybody's house in Miami will last. These curtains are replaced every ten years because of air-conditioning, but materials don't last, books on paper don't last." Mr. Wolfson is meeting the challenge head-on, and has installed state-of-the-art systems for climate control and an insect-free environment for his precious libraries, both at home and in his museum. This means that from time to time he has to close his house entirely for fumigation purposes.

As he adds to his collections he sees himself as an agent for scholars and librarians, acquiring books and objects for their use. "I give them the material and they shape the vessel," he says with modesty. He himself uses the word "propagate" for his role in leading people to his sources of knowledge, a typically provocative image from this unusual bibliophile.

The joy Mitchell Wolfson derives from his collections springs not only from their power to enlarge people's perceptions but also from their aesthetic nature. He looks at books as objects containing not only the text, but also a visual message. "Today the image is more powerful than the word. I'm considered old-fashioned because although I respond to images, they are the nineteenth-century images of lithographs and old letterpress techniques rather than photography or computer printing."

The ultimate power of visual images is, of course, propaganda, so it is natural enough that Mr. Wolfson publishes a *Journal of Decorative and Propaganda Arts,* which contains articles about religious art, political posters, advertising, and other subjects related to this topic. "I love illustrations, I love what they tell us. I love the adventure of reading and the relationships with other people that I have within a book, and I love the frozen, slowed-down time provided by reading so that one can have greater pleasure from it. I know no other way." ↢

English Country House Libraries

From the fourteenth century, most feudal lords of English manors could read, and by the sixteenth century most had a collection of a dozen to a hundred books. But it was not until the eighteenth century that it became fashionable to have a special room designed exclusively for books. By that time, aristocratic rivalry for the highest artistic and literary reputation was reflected in the amount of paintings and books, and quality of library design, that the gentlemen aesthetes could build for themselves. The results produced some of the finest rooms in Europe.

These are examples of the great architect-designers of that brilliant century—Robert Adam's work at Kedleston Hall in Derbyshire, that of his rival, William Kent, at Holkham Hall, in Norfolk, and of James Wyatt at Belvoir Castle in Leicestershire. The other libraries are at Longleat House in Wiltshire (which dates from the sixteenth century, but was rebuilt after a series of fires) and Badminton House in Gloucestershire.

right

A PLATE OF GLASS ON TOP OF A PILE OF BOOKS

MAKES A UTILITARIAN COFFEE TABLE.

above

BREATHTAKING PROPORTIONS DAZZLE THE EYE IN WILLIAM

KENT'S MASTERPIECE AT HOLKHAM HALL, NORFOLK.

left

A FOLIO STAND AT HOLKHAM DISPLAYS ONE OF THE

LIBRARY'S MANY TREASURES.

left

ROBERT ADAMS WAS THE ARCHITECT OF THIS ELEGANT LIBRARY AT KEDLESTON HALL IN DERBYSHIRE.

below left

ELEGANT ARCHES ADD DEPTH TO THE BISHOP'S LIBRARY AT LONGLEAT.

51

Hay-on-Wye—Booktown

Take a beautiful, remote, unspoiled village in the mountainous landscape along the border of England and Wales. Add the energy, entrepreneurial spirit, and bibliomanic enthusiasm of one man, Richard Booth. The result: the only village in Britain that has more bookshops than pubs, and probably the only village in the world whose international fame and tourist business rest not on architecture, art, sports, or restaurants but on those innocent rectangular objects called books.

Hay-on-Wye is a booklovers' theme park. Its twenty-seven new and secondhand bookshops scattered up and down its narrow streets, its outdoor bookstands and shelves, its bookbinders, printshops, auctions, and special events, lure thousands of book buyers, book dealers, and just plain tourists from all over the world.

Perhaps the most famous attraction in Hay-on-Wye is the Cinema Bookshop on Castle Street, which is literally a converted movie house, now jam-packed with over 250,000 books where the seats used to be and offering as magical an experience as any projected onto the silver screen. Outside, rows of book bins provide a bewildering mix of literary delights, all

left

WINDOWS, WALLS, TILES, SIGNS—ALL
SPEAK OF BOOKS IN HAY-ON-WYE.

above

CHARMING TIMBERED STOREFRONTS ACT AS

BACKDROPS TO THIS LITERARY MARKETPLACE.

of the books priced at fifty pence. In front of these book bins, a strange glass pyramid, straight out of an episode of *Star Trek,* adds to the surreal quality of what the local guidebooks call the most A-Maze-Ing Bookshop in the World.

The founder of this reader's paradise, Richard Booth, lives fittingly in the castle at the top of the hill. His family has lived in the area since the 1880s. His father, an army officer with a penchant for reading, used to take his son into secondhand bookshops, igniting the boy's interest in the business. "The great thing about secondhand dealers," Mr. Booth says, "is that they vary from being failed actors to retired merchant seamen. We are not professionals, but came to books each in our own way."

Richard Booth's passion for books and flair for marketing inspired the idea of a "book town." He sees it as a way of saving from extinction old towns and villages abandoned in the flight to the supermarket. As he says, "The secondhand book trade is a rural economy—and it operates year-round." Nicolas Barker, book expert and National Trust

libraries curator, agrees that the secondhand book business, once a lame duck in the industry, is now flourishing. "When the high street bookshop disappeared, thanks to the invasion of the big book chains, book dealers retired to rectories where they could go on dealing in a genteel fashion. But people gradually saw that old books were not only made better and lasted longer than new ones, particularly paperbacks, but secondhand hardbacks were often great bargains, since new book prices have skyrocketed in the last ten to fifteen years. So the secondhand book business suddenly became profitable, and is now growing fast."

Hay-on-Wye is living proof of Mr. Booth's vision and Mr. Barker's diagnosis. Crowds of people come every year to Hay to browse, to examine, to buy. Mr. Booth is now helping create book towns all over Europe, and even in America—Stillwater, for instance, on the borders of Wisconsin and Minnesota. "Today's libraries can't cope with the books they have to keep available," Richard Booth declares. "The future of the book is in book towns." ↷

above

EVEN THE BED-AND-BREAKFAST SIGN

HAS A BOOKLOVER'S THEME.

BEAUTIFUL
BOOKSCAPES

Visually Inspired Libraries

IF I WERE BLIND, I WOULD STILL

TAKE PLEASURE IN HOLDING A

BEAUTIFUL BOOK. ∾

—SYLVESTER DE SARCY

LAURIE MALLET

RENZO MONGIARDINO

THERESE AND ERWIN HARRIS

THOMAS BRITT

RICHARD MINSKY

MICHELE OKA DONER

TIMOTHY MAWSON

"BIBLIOTHÈQUE," TROMPE L'OEIL WALLPAPER DESIGNED BY
RICHARD NEAS FOR BRUNSCHWIG & FILS.

Laurie Mallet

"A ROOM FILLED WITH MEMORIES OF THE PAST."

What is a library but a room full of memories? Here, where designer Laurie Mallet lives with her family, the whole house is a storehouse of memories. Any changes made to this 1820 landmark townhouse in New York's Greenwich Village, redolent of history, required the greatest tact. Alison Sky, of the design firm SITE, saw the walls of the house as planes between the past and the present, and worked all her architectural changes with this paradigm in mind.

The library is on the second floor of the house, part of a living space that was once two separate rooms. The whole room, including the floor, is painted white—even some of the books themselves. On the library wall, white books float out of the shelves like ghostly images, unmarked, unidentified, books of the imagination. The backs of other books may be seen pressing up against the wall as though peeking through the next-door house, making a visual connection with other worlds and other times. Merging with these dreamlike volumes (which could represent whatever favorite books we remember best) are Laurie Mallet's real books, which she reads for work and pleasure, witness to a very vivid present.

Nothing is trompe l'oeil here. The white books are real books, painted white. They have authentic spines and bindings. They can be moved or stacked. The only thing unreal about them is that they cannot be opened or read. They were treated with a resin that made them solid, and painted with the same paint that covers the wall and the bookshelves. These are closed books, containing, in effect, recollections of reading.

For Laurie Mallet, there were practical considerations supporting Alison Sky's innovative vision. The book wall covers up pipes for plumbing and air-conditioning. The shelves are generously high and wide to accept her large collection of oversize art, architecture, and design books. Ms. Mallet admits to no organizational plan. She grew up in Paris in a house filled with books, and finds in her own, much smaller house in New York that there is not enough room for them. They have spread to the floor both here and in other rooms, other spaces.

Ms. Mallet sees her second-floor library as symbolic, just as Alison Sky sees it. "With these mysterious white books, the room is filled with memories of the past," Alison Sky says. "Laurie's own books fill in the spaces, bringing it into the present." ∾

opposite

A SYMBOLIC LIBRARY OF ALL-WHITE BINDINGS RUBS UP AGAINST
THE COLORFUL JACKETS OF A DESIGNER'S PERSONAL COLLECTION.

Renzo Mongiardino

"The library as theater"

What is a library of not a place in which to dream? Given the right artist/architect, a room for books in a modern American city may be catapulted into European history and the fortunate reader surrounded by visual stimuli normally available only in the mind's eye.

In the New York apartment of the late Peter Sharp, the Italian designer Renzo Mongiardino created a library and reading room that seems to have been transported from a Renaissance palace. A famous trompe l'oeil specialist, Mongiardino conceived of a library situated on a rooftop terrace rather than inside a room. To this end he painted soaring vistas of the city's skyline on the walls, the buildings and trees hallucinatory, like ghosts.

The furniture of this library, however, is far from illusory. A magnificent central desk, based on a design by Michelangelo, dominates the room. A monumental reading easel and bookcase, large enough to house oversize volumes, and leather-bound armchairs keep the room firmly anchored in reality. In an anteroom to the main reading room, a bookcase designed with a Palladian facade and trompe l'oeil marble inlay anticipates the architectural theme that pervades this space.

Renzo Mongiardino was trained in architecture and design, and soon gained a reputation for dramatic and theatrical interiors. He became a set and film designer (for Zeffirelli's *Romeo and Juliet*, for instance) and refined his skills in trompe l'oeil. He has made no secret of the fact that his favorite period is the Italian Renaissance, admiring particularly the Villa Giulia and the Piazza Navona, both in Rome. This New York library is a splendid example of the designer's tastes and talents. ❧

opposite

BEHIND A MAHOGANY LECTERN AND BOOKCASE, A COMBINATION OF ANCIENT AND MODERN BUILDINGS PAINTED IN THE BACKGROUND REACHES FOR THE SKY.

right

WITH THE POWER OF RENZO MONGIARDINO'S ILLUSION, IT SEEMS AS THOUGH A RENAISSANCE MUSICIAN RECENTLY SAT STRUMMING IN THE SUNLIT ARMCHAIR.

below

SURROUNDED BY FANTASTIC VARIATIONS ON NEW YORK CITY'S SKYLINE PAINTED LIKE FRESCOES ON THE WALLS, THE MICHELANGELO-INSPIRED DESK REIGNS SUPREME.

Therese and Erwin Harris

"BOOKS ARE LIKE WORKS OF ART. YOU ENJOY THEM, YOU'RE THEIR GUARDIANS

FOR A WHILE, YOU'RE AWARE THAT OTHER PEOPLE HAVE OWNED AND ENJOYED

THEM FOR A SHORT TIME, AND THEN THEY ARE PASSED ON."

You must call ahead from the mainland to reconfirm time of arrival. You wait for clearance to board an auto ferry that transports you to Florida's reclusive retreat, Fisher Island. A security escort drives invited visitors to the Harris Villa for a private viewing of a scholar's library.

The Harris home is sheltered from the sun with a climate-controlled atmosphere. Its cool, darkened interior protects a research library that supports the rare collection of antiquities Erwin and Therese Harris have been assembling for half a century, devoted to ancient art from northern China, southern Siberia, and Central Asia.

Two ceramic horses from the Tang dynasty are symbolic gatekeepers guarding a thousand-volume library, encompassed within five walls of a relatively small house. A light-riveting glass vault, framed in bronze, is centered in a custom-built bookwall. It encases a treasury of jade and bronze art objects and is the magnetic force that draws you into a cul de sac for viewing and study.

Shang bronze ceremonial vessels, more than three thousand years old, are buttressed with books on archaeology and the Bronze Age published in Chinese, French, Russian, and English. *The World of the Huns, Frozen Tombs of Siberia,* and *Cultural Frontiers in Ancient East Asia* are a few of the visible titles. "My books record the disparate cultures of China and the warrior horsemen of the Great Steppes, those 'barbarians' the Great Wall was built to keep out," Erwin explains. "A lot of research became available only in the last decade through increased archaeological work in China."

Recent research helped the Harrises identify a five-thousand year-old jade pendant that Erwin discovered at an estate sale in the 1960s. Realizing its historic value, the Harrises donated this rare example of late Neolithic Chinese culture to the Freer Gallery in 1993. Emma Bunker, co-curator with Dr. Jenny So of a Smithsonian exhibition featuring a hundred pieces from the Harris collection, is one of the many Asian art specialists who do research in the Harrises' library.

"Whenever I visit, I spend as much time looking at their books as I do the art," Bunker reveals. "Therese and Erwin have built a remarkable library for their collection. Their books put their art pieces into

opposite

A BRONZE-FRAMED GLASS VAULT DISPLAYS ANCIENT BRONZE AND
JADE PIECES. THEIR HISTORY AND THE CULTURES THEY REPRESENT
ARE DESCRIBED IN THE SURROUNDING VOLUMES.

above

A JOSEF HOFFMAN TABLE AND FLEDERMAUS CHAIRS FROM A CAFÉ
IN VIENNA. ASIAN ART SPECIALISTS AND MUSEUM CURATORS WHO
DO RESEARCH IN THE HARRIS LIBRARY WORK HERE.

top

"TOOTHED" JADE PENDANT DONATED BY THE HARRISES TO THE
FREER GALLERY. UNDISCOVERED UNTIL THE LATE 1970'S, IT IS THE
GALLERY'S ONLY ARTIFACT FROM THE RECENTLY IDENTIFIED
HONGSHAN CULTURE OF THE NEOLITHIC PERIOD, C. 3500–3000 B.C.

below left

A CORBUSIER CHAISE IS A FAVORITE READING PLACE FOR ERWIN
AND THERESE.

below right

THE HARRISES READING ON A VERANDA A HUNDRED FEET FROM THE
WATER'S EDGE. THEIR VILLA PROVIDES A SERENITY THAT COMPLEMENTS
THEIR COLLECTION OF ASIAN ART AND RARE BOOKS.

chronological context. They record the times in which they were created, the taste of a particular age, and the history of ownership, right up to the present. It's wonderful to find a collector who is also a scholar."

Therese and Erwin's books, like their art, have a personal history all their own. "We have major scholarly books that are autographed or inscribed with the names of previous owners," Erwin says. "A lot of our books are from generations of other people. Books are like works of art. You enjoy them, you're their guardians for a while, you're aware that other people have owned them, enjoyed them for a short time, and then they are passed on, touched by other hands."

The Harrises are protective of the books they've been collecting for more than four decades. "I'm the only one who handles the books and I do so very carefully because so many of them are rare and fragile. We don't lend books, but if people, such as museum curators, want information, they can tell me what they need and I'll photocopy it for them," Erwin says.

A member of the International Council of Museums' Committee for the Conservation of Works of Art, Erwin has taken every precaution to safeguard their collection. "Because of the Florida climate we have the air conditioner on almost all of the time, even in the storage bunker, where we keep books and objects not on exhibition or displayed in our library. We monitor the humidity carefully. All the windows are coated with a special ultraviolet protective film and we never expose rooms to direct sunlight. The house and display cases are all protected by a state-of-the-art alarm system, essential when you have a collection of this historic value." ✑

Thomas Britt

"Books Do Furnish a Room"

In this case, "furnish," as in the title of Anthony Powell's novel, is not too strong a word. Books have been called on to play a vital part in the design of this large and glamorous living room belonging to interior designer Thomas Britt.

The room has been through many changes. Originally it had an Oriental flavor, with the banquettes covered in lacquer-red fabric and four Chinese Chippendale étagères reminiscent of England's Brighton Pavilion as bookshelves. But for its most recent incarnation, Mr. Britt has resorted to the palest of palettes. To that end every object of furniture in the room, every piece of fabric, every sliver of gilding, every chip of wood, has been selected with microscopic attention as to its shape and color.

But in a design as controlled as this, the asymmetrical sizes and dissonant colors exhibited by book jackets would be as out of place as a jazz band in a monastery. "They were too jarring," Mr. Britt decided. So he collected up the books and reupholstered them in uniform bindings to harmonize with the rest of his very carefully coordinated design. "I slipcovered them, as was the custom in seventeenth-century libraries such as the one in Prague, where books were covered in parchment," he says. Thus, firmly bound in shiny cream-colored paper (available in any good paper store) and identified with gold-framed handwritten labels, his newly disciplined volumes are arranged in horizontal piles in the pagoda-shaped étagères.

Thomas Britt has come up with one other clever idea—he has wrapped his magazines in the same paper, several issues contained in one creamy binding, neatly solving the messy problem of magazine storage, and yet making them easily accessible for consultation. ✑

opposite

MAGAZINES AND BOOKS LIE SIDE BY SIDE IN HORIZONTAL HARMONY, UNIFIED BY THEIR ELEGANT SLIPCOVERS.

overleaf

IN THIS SUBTLY LIT ROOM OF MUTED COLORS, THE BOOKS IN THEIR CREAMY STACKS HAVE BEEN GIVEN A VITAL DECORATIVE ROLE.

Richard Minsky

"The message is not 'read this book' but 'see this book.'"

Richard Minsky, founder of the Center for Book Arts in New York City, is a scholar turned printer and bookbinder. He creates book bindings for every occasion and purpose—weddings, guest books, museum exhibitions, poetry, personal gifts. Each one is a work of art in itself, designed, tooled, sewn, and finished by this fast-talking, fast-thinking polymath in a small studio in Greenwich Village or on his boat off Long Island. In 1972 he started a bindery and printshop in Forest Hills, expanding to the nonprofit Center for Book Arts in Manhattan in 1974, a place where people may study the arts of printing, bookbinding, and restoration, and create their own books.

"Both my parents died when I was young, so I needed supplementary income to make my way through life. I started printing early, when I was in junior high school, inspired by my graphic arts teacher. I bought a small printing press, started a printing business, and hired my homeroom class as a sales team. I made money with my little handpress all through high school and college.

"I graduated from Brooklyn College in economics and won a fellowship to Brown University. There, in the Ann Mary Brown Memorial Room, I found two thousand incunabula (books printed before 1501). The curator came in and saw me with them and asked, 'You like the books?' I said, 'Both books and bindings.' So he sent me to Dan Knowlton at the university bindery. I loved the place so I took his extension course on bookbinding and then spent all my days in his bindery.

"By 1969 I started working for the Hirshhorn Museum, in New York at that time. I started binding books for them, mostly art books. In this way I obtained my art education. Handling all that art, some of it rubbed off on me. I realized they had no books that were artworks in themselves, so I began to make bindings that qualified as art. Later I started exhibiting my bindings in art galleries and museums. I saw there was a need for a studio-based organization that went beyond the traditional ideas of bookbinding, so I founded the Center for Book Arts.

"My passion for bookbinding originated in the feel, the smell, the actual physical object of the book. I love the process of producing it with my hands. Printing doesn't involve the same kind of manual dexterity. Some of my earliest bindings are horrible. It took me years to bind books well.

"My own collection reflects my belief in the mysterious power of books. When you read, it's not only the feel and the look of the book that stimulates you, it's the vibes the book has absorbed from its history over the years. That's why I collected old books for so long. I was struck by this when I was studying at Brown. I had always been interested in Adam Smith, had read his *Wealth of Nations* a couple of times, and owned several editions. But the copy at Brown was the 1776 (first) edition, and it was inscribed with the name of the then finance minister of France. Now that was of particular importance to me, because when I was doing my research on the origins of Adam Smith's thought, I discovered he was influenced by certain French philosophers and 'physiocrats' (none of whom had been translated) as well as by English thinkers like Jeremy Bentham and the Utilitarians, who most scholars thought were his ideological predecessors. So I started reading this book that had been held by the finance minister of France and all at once I was transformed back into 1776. As I read, suddenly I had a whole different conception of what Adam Smith was writing about. All the vibes started coming into my hands and completely changed my understanding of the book.

"So then I started collecting books, even some in languages I didn't read, just on the basis of the vibes I got holding them. That became the basis of my collection—books with vibes.

"Now I collect books as objects, where the case and binding are a metaphor to the text, such as a book on tobacco bound like a cigar box. I have become fascinated with the iconographic, totemic nature of bindings as artifacts. The books I bind go into museums and exhibitions and the message is not '*read* this book' but '*see* this book.'

"I look for books with specific subject matter that interests me, such as politics, the environment, individual freedom, and so on. If, by the binding, I can draw attention to material that I think is important and has been neglected, I feel I have accomplished something. As far as I am concerned, that is what bookbinding is about."

S O M E   O F   R I C H A R D   M I N S K Y ' S   B I N D I N G S

PETTIGREW'S HISTORY OF EGYPTIAN MUMMIES

FAMILY ALBUM

THE CRISIS OF DEMOCRACY

RICHARD MINSKY AT WORK IN HIS BINDERY IN NEW YORK. THE
VOLUME IS A VISITOR'S BOOK FOR AN INTERNATIONAL CLIENT,
BOUND IN LEATHER WITH VERMEIL CLASPS.

For instance, the book entitled *The Crisis of Democracy* is wrapped in barbed wire as a metaphor to represent the author's thesis that there is too much personal freedom in contemporary democracies and that it should be curtailed to preserve governability. The wire springs back to become a reading stand for the book. "It is important that a binding work well, both to protect the text and be readable."

Guest Book for Gracie Mansion, commissioned by the Gracie Mansion Conservancy, was set in chains to prevent theft. The book is dedicated to all mayors for generations to come. Mayor Ed Koch wrote the dedication and then, according to Mr. Minsky, took the book home with him when he left office. "You can see why he wanted it, but it wasn't made for him, it was made for the mayors of the City of New York. Still, I'm very happy when people steal my books."

Mr. Minsky also created book bindings made out of snakeskin, the skins once belonging to a

Spanish nobleman. "Working with them, I started discovering where tribal cultures got their images. When cut, the patterns of the snakeskins generate this imagery—it magically appears before your eyes. Of course bindings, like books by the yard, can be used to decorate people's libraries, but that's a nineteenth-century idea. I think the function of bookbinding in the twentieth century is to turn the book into an icon or totem of the particular text, that may inspire people to buy the actual book and read it. It goes beyond decorative art, it relates to art and politics and communication." ☙

MISSILE ENVY (WITH LIVE ROCKETS)

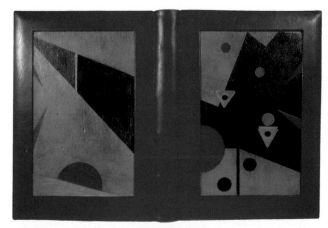

A BOOK WITH INLAID SNAKESKIN

Michele Oka Doner

"BOOKS ARE CENTRAL TO OUR LIFE; THE LIBRARY IS THE HEART

OF OUR HOUSE."

I've always treasured books, from the time I was a child. I lived near a wonderful public library in Miami Beach that was built of keystone eulytite, so not only did I like the books, I remember liking the building. I must have been five. Every Saturday I would walk from my house through a park of beautiful banyan trees. I was allowed to take out two books and then I could return them and take out two more. It was a very important part of my life. There was no television in those days.

"I was encouraged to read when I was very young. I had my own bookcases and they were filled with books like *Heidi* and *Madeline*. In those days storytelling was something people still did, so when my grandfather baby-sat for us on Sunday nights, he would tell us wonderful stories. I didn't understand what a Russian tradition this was until I read Maxim Gorky's *My Childhood*.

"Both my father and grandfather came from Vilna. They were 'scribes' who were called upon to read and write for those who could not. These learned men passed on their love of books, writing, and 'the word' to me. Word symbolism has influenced and inspired many of my designs and artworks. They also probably contributed to my ability to reduce images to glyphs (icons or pictographs) as I did for the library in Sacramento and I am now doing for the International Airport in Miami.

"The treasures that seeded my library came from my husband's family. Frederick's grandfather had a wonderful house in Shaker Heights, Ohio, filled with many remarkable books from his childhood in the 1800s. We inherited a signed Mark Twain *Following the Equator;* a great book on Napoleon's victories, inscribed to Frederick's grandfather in 1895; a leather-bound second edition of *Webster's Dictionary;* and *Gulliver's Travels.* The

opposite

MICHELE OKA DONER CLIMBS A TWELVE-FOOT ROLLING LADDER
DAILY TO REACH VOLUMES ON TOP SHELVES OF HER "BOOK TOWER"
LIBRARY. CENTER STAGE: A BUGATTI CEREMONIAL CHAIR. VINTAGE
BINDINGS AND POP CULTURE BOOK JACKETS CREATE A BACKDROP
OF STACCATO COLOR.

library of music books were a legacy from my husband's grandmother, a pianist and opera lover.

"Our library is a blending of three different families and five generations. One of my favorite things in it is the *Children of the World* series published by the Encyclopaedia Britannica in 1947. I've also kept several books from my childhood and they are here along with the core of the collection that came from our grandparents. As I developed profes-

sionally, I added books on architecture, design, ancient art, archaeology, and anthropology. Then there were also all those books on music that reflected my husband's passion, that had been in another area of the house. I decided it should all come together. I liked the idea of the library as the heart of the house, which is why we centered it in the loft space. Now when you go into the library, books surround you. There's something wonderful about going into a three-dimensional space with books higher than you are, as you remember they were in the stacks at college. I decided to organize my 'book tower' as a research and reference library. Books are central to our life so they have their own centered place in our home.

"We decided to paint the library black at the last minute. Initially we thought it should be maple so it would seem to grow out of the floor. But we risked darkening it because the loft is large and white and we wanted the library to emerge in stark contrast to it. I like the yin-and-yang atmosphere it creates. The black grid frames the books, containing them and providing a counterpoint to colorful book jackets and classic book bindings.

"When I started planning this library I was amazed at what I had. I didn't lay it out formally but organized it in sections. A first section would be devoted to Oriental art and culture. Another would

above left

LEAVES OF AN OPEN BOOK, ONE OF THREE HUNDRED SYMBOLIC BRONZE INLAYS MICHELE DESIGNED FOR THE FLOOR OF THE SACRAMENTO CENTRAL LIBRARY.

left

AN EIGHTEENTH-DYNASTY (1567–1320 B.C.) LIMESTONE EGYPTIAN MEMORIAL TABLET FROM THE TOMB OF NOBLEWOMAN IAHHOTPI.

opposite, top

A STAINLESS-STEEL BOOK JACKET SHELTERS SYLVANUS MORLEY'S
ANCIENT MAYA, ONE OF A CUSTOM-WELDED COLLECTION OF BOOKS
ASSEMBLED BY A DETROIT AUTO EXECUTIVE. A CUBAN CIGAR
MAKER'S CEDAR BOX HOUSES A BOOK ON ARTIST JOSEPH CORNELL,
GIFTS OF DESIRE, A LIMITED EDITION BY DICKRAN TASHIAN.

below

HUNDREDS OF *NATIONAL GEOGRAPHICS* THAT DATE BACK TO 1919
WERE THE CATALYST FOR DONER'S LIBRARY. A BLACK GRID MADE OF
STANDARD READY-TO-ASSEMBLE SHELVES IS ANCHORED TO A WALL
STRONG ENOUGH TO SUPPORT HER ARCHIVE.

be reserved for books on Western civilization and the
pre-Columbian era. Sections for literature, poetry,
and etymology would fit into the eight-inch shelves
at the top. The newest section would make additional
room for art history, design, and photography
because so much of what I am doing now requires
research on art in public places, urban planning,
architecture, and nature.

"I don't need a computer to find the books I
have. It's all in my head. I can get my hands on anything in two minutes. I use our library ladder almost
every day. I'll sit in my Bugatti chair, reading and
enjoying the space. At other times I will bring my
books to the couch in the retreat alcove I call my
reading room. I *never* read in bed!

"Our accountant nearly dropped dead when he

THE FLORIDA HOUSE

saw what I spent on books last year. My husband said: 'I guess he doesn't know too many people who would spend more money on books than clothes.'

"I edit my library from time to time. Some books you keep, others you pass on to friends, family, young people who can't afford expensive books. My library is always evolving. It's as an organic entity.

"I'm creating a whole new book environment in our Florida home. I didn't want to repeat or deplete our library in New York and so it has a very different focus and ambiance. It's less structured and less serious. I wanted it to represent the complete change that this second home is for us. Instead of building a system of bookshelves I have a sixty-foot platform, three-and-a-half-feet wide, that runs under the window. I didn't want to put anything up on the walls that would compete with the panoramic view.

"It's logical that the books in our second library should concentrate on Florida. It's where I grew up." ❧

BEACHCOMBER, SCAVENGER, SCULPTOR, ARTIST, AND BIBLIOPHILE, MICHELE POSITIONS BOOKS ON THE EVERGLADES AND THE FLORA AND FAUNA OF THE CARRIBEAN WITH OBJECTS AND SHELLS COLLECTED ON HER DAILY WALKS ALONG THE SHORE.

OKA DONER'S LIBRARIES HAVE A STRONG SENSE OF PLACE. IN CONTRAST TO A TOWER LIBRARY THAT EVOKES MANHATTAN, HER PLATFORM LIBRARY IN FLORIDA MIRRORS THE BEACHSCAPE VIEW, PRESERVED BY ORGANIZING BOOKS BELOW THE WINDOW LINE. TWO CAST BRONZE CHAIRS SHE SCULPTED ARE IN THE FOREGROUND.

Timothy Mawson

"I WOULD NEVER HAVE A ROOM WITHOUT BOOKS.

THEY'RE A TRANSFORMING ELEMENT."

My books are my friends, they're like family to me. There are some books I've opened only once or twice within the last five years, but I would never part with them because they're part of me. They were very, very carefully selected and I've had some of them for more than twenty-five years. I wouldn't sell them unless I needed to, as I did when I first got started." Timothy Mawson, garden book collector, dealer, and writer, started as a bookseller in New York before setting up shop, and home, in New Preston, Connecticut.

Mawson needs little coaxing to talk about the books he surrounds himself with in his eighteenth-century garden-tour house and country store, Timothy Mawson's Books and Prints. "I enjoy books as physical objects," he says. "I love to hold a book in my hand, the feel of the paper, the beauty of its typography and illustrations, the design of its pages, and, yes, the book jacket, all of it! I've often picked up a book because its dustcover was just so beautiful. If I had to choose between having a wall of paintings and a wall of books, I would certainly choose books. When you walk into a room of books, you're embraced by them. They're a transforming element."

Books arc in constant view in Mawson's home, from the book wall you see immediately on entering his living room/library to the staircase you climb to reach his cloistered bedroom, where he reveals his collection of illustrated books from the 1930s and '40s. "Illustrated books are my main crush," Mawson reveals, "because books from this period are unsurpassed in design. They had a whimsy and a charm you rarely see in books and book jackets today. That's why there's such a demand for them."

Mawson is especially proud of the collection he's kept of Denton Welsh, who illustrated his own books from endpaper to endpaper. Complete works by Welsh, Cecil Beaton, and, Mawson's favorite, Rex

opposite

CECIL BEATON'S *DIARIES* WITH OTHER VINTAGE VOLUMES
MAWSON SHELTERS IN A SPECIALLY DESIGNED BOOK ALCOVE
IN HIS BEDROOM.

overleaf

MAWSON HAS CREATED GARDEN-BOOK STILL-LIFES IN HIS SHOP
WITH BOTANICAL PRINTS, ANTIQUE GARDEN TOOLS, OLD SEED
CATALOGS, AND WEATHERED ATTIC ARTIFACTS.

Whistler, illuminate the the room. "I suppose I'm being rather greedy by keeping all these wonderful books up here. I've also held on to several very beautiful botanical books from the seventeenth century because I know they'll be broken up for plates if I sell them." A book collector as well as a dealer, Mawson is often conflicted about selling his treasures. "Selling books is really a second career," he says.

Mawson was drawn to gardening books and horticulture through scouting trips to England spurred by personal requests from friends. "Many were keen gardeners and gave me lists of books that weren't available in this country, books by William Robinson, Gertrude Jekyll, Vita Sackville-West, and E. A. Bowles. It just snowballed from there."

Mawson has a reputation for creating "book collages" and reading-room environments. "When you look at a room," he says, "you automatically know where books belong. There are logical places and spaces for them. I have books in most of the rooms in my house; some fill the shelves of a book wall; others are protected by and clearly embellish the wood cabinets they're in; others rest on chairs, inviting reading, browsing, borrowing, or, when I transport them to my shop, buying, I hope."

A self-defined visual person, Mawson points out that books are enhanced when they are interspersed with other objects of beauty: porcelains, statuary, memory-evoking photographs and postcards. "Even when I first began I would bring a lot of accessories from home into my shop and use them as props for book displays," Mawson says. "They weren't for sale then but my customers inevitably wanted to buy them. All the things I love are in my shop today in one form or another. They are extensions of myself. For me, bookselling is a personal business." ℘

opposite, top

A VIEW OF THE CECIL BEATON *DIARIES* MAWSON COVETS AS MUCH

FOR THEIR DUST JACKETS AS FOR THEIR REVELATIONS.

opposite, bottom

A SAMPLING OF THE VINTAGE BOOKS MAWSON COLLECTS.

above

THE LIVING ROOM IN MAWSON'S COUNTRY HOME DOUBLES AS A

LIBRARY/READING ROOM FURNISHED WITH A CUPBOARD-STYLE

BOOK CABINET, BODY-HUGGING READING CHAIRS, AND A

NINETEENTH-CENTURY AMERICAN EMPIRE SECRETAIRE.

How to Organize Your Library

You have a few, maybe a hundred, maybe thousands of books. Books you grew up with, books you have saved over the years, books you've been given, books you can't bear to throw away. Where do they go? Where is the one you were just reading? Why is there no more shelf space? Why can't you find the one you need most? What are those piles on the floor?

Enter the library organizer, the person who examines your books and tells you where they should be arranged, and what you should keep. There are such people, both amateur and professional, but the man who has worked on some of the most interesting libraries in the United States (including those of Diana Vreeland, Brooke Astor, Leslie Wexner, and Leonard Lauder) is Kurt Thometz, whose company, The Private Library, in Brooklyn, New York, provides services that most book people only dream of. "When I enter a library," he says, "the sensibility of the owner almost immediately reveals itself. Then it is simply a matter of responding to that sensibility."

Kurt Thometz recommends the following procedure for the despairing bibliophile. His secrets, revealed below, will help solve the ever-present and everlasting problem of all readers—how to live happily ever after with their books.

On Shelving the Library

1   After making a thorough search of the premises, break down the books into categories by subject matter: fiction and literature, arts and crafts, cookbooks and gardening, history and economics, etc. Compare their quantities to the available shelf space. If necessary, measure. Consider the book's height as well as its width. You may need to adjust your shelves to optimize your space.

2   Attend to their distribution. Consider the function of the room in relationship to the content of its shelves. Books serve several functions and should be placed where they will come to hand when needed. Reference books, for instance, should be as near to your desk as possible, just as the book you're reading should be by the easy chair or nightstand.

    If you have bookshelves in the living room, I suggest putting your picture books there, so that visitors can pick them up and look at them without losing track of the conversation in the room. In a social context, better in a public space than showing off your literary first editions, which people cannot look at without concentrating, is to have what some book snobs refer to as *non-books,* books that aren't meant to be read; fine bindings, exquisite print jobs, large format art and photography books that have little or no text.

    Useful books have their obvious places; cookbooks in the kitchen, gardening books near the entrance to the garden. A guest room's shelves require a bit more resource. Nothing makes guests feel more comfortable than a choice from their host's books. Particularly good are commonplace books and anthologies, short stories, curiosities, and children's books.

Give serious consideration to the bedroom. Years ago a West Coast rare book dealer compiled a collection of books on the themes of love and romance that I would like to see in my wife's boudoir.

    Consider the architecture of the room. If it is designed in a particular style, such as Art Deco, books relating to that period would fit in very well. If it is a light, open or glassed-in space, a collection of illustrated or garden books can be well displayed there. A dark, cozy room calls for books that offer more personal and intimate subject matters.

3   Once you have distributed the books to their rooms and on the shelves, put them in order. Where it seems that alphabetical order won't suffice, create an order and see how it works.

    Some subjects adhere to alphabetical order. Fiction takes to it best. Literature can frequently be shelved with all fiction titles, unless it comprises a collection unto itself. For instance, literary biography or criticism can be shelved with the author's works, poetry and belles lettres mixed in. An author's collected works might be placed in chronological order within the alphabetical order.

    Other subjects require the process of association. History, for instance, does not shelve well by author. One of the better examples of how to shelve history is Alastair Cooke's library of American history, which is arranged geographically, Maine in the upper right-hand corner, California in the lower left, etc. Chronological order, of course, works well within this subject.

On Thinning Out the Library

In my line of work this is a very sensitive issue. It needs addressing when a library has either outgrown its shelf space or is moving to smaller quarters. One never knows another person's association with a book. *Jonathan Livingston Seagull* may indeed have changed somebody's life.

1   The first books to go are out-of-date travel guides. They are obsolete almost immediately and tend to take up a lot of space.

2   Self-help books. Their usefulness tends to become dated as people and psychological fashions change.

3   Trashy novels. In general there is very little interest in popular literature once it has fallen off the best-seller list, as it is not worth anybody's time to reread it. (That is the generality. It is also true that many writers who should be read today aren't because they were so popular in their time. John O'Hara's novels fall into this category.)

4   Quality literature in mass-market paperback format. When space is at a premium, I suggest you throw out the books that are always going to be easy to get. When you want to reread *War and Peace,* it will only be as far as the nearest bookshop or public library.

Remember that weeding out a library is a constant process. Every year one accumulates books, and every year one's books should be re-evaluated.

4   As you put the books in order, arrange them. Shelf height will dictate whether they stand up straight or lie on their sides. There is essentially nothing wrong with stacking books on top of each other, but it does make them more difficult to get at, especially on an upper shelf.

Leave space for new books as you go along. You'll find the empty spaces ideal for small vases or objects. The better you can anticipate where you'll be adding books in the future, the longer your overall arrangement will last. You may have to go back over a section and take in or let out that space, but this way you have the best chance of leaving some room.

On Disposing of Unwanted Books

Where do we take the books we have weeded out or wish to throw away? Used books can be sold to used book dealers or given to church sales, charities, hospitals, prisons, schools, as well as libraries. If you give to charity, write down the title, author, and price of the book. It is tax-deductible. Some charities will assess the value for you and give you a receipt. If the books you are discarding don't seem worth the bother, leave them outside on a city street. They will almost certainly disappear within days.

Final Advice

The one mistake almost all of us make, including library designers and collectors, according to Natalie Bauman of Bauman Rare Books, is *not making enough space for the library to expand.* "I think it is imperative to assume that your library is going to grow beyond what you or your architect anticipates. Many collectors who built their libraries early in their collecting careers, and many people who simply love books, are terribly sorry that they had not considered space for expansion."

above

ORDERLY BOOKSHELVES REFLECT AN ORDERLY MIND—IN THIS CASE, BELONGING TO IRISH HISTORIAN AND AUTHOR DESMOND GUINNESS.

above

CLEVER SPACE-SAVING: BOOKSHELVES TUCKED UNDER THE STAIRS AND BUILT INTO A LANDING WALL SOLVE BOOK-STORAGE PROBLEMS IN A SMALL AREA.

How to Start a Collection

THE BOOK ∘ ALAN PRYCE JONES

I f you would like to be a collector, and you need for space or financial reasons to start small, a good way to begin, says Natalie Bauman of Bauman Rare Books, is to select a specialized field (medicine, science, literature, history, law exploration), a period (the American Revolution, the ancient world, the eighteenth century), a movement (women's studies, African-American history), or a theme. This way you can amass a comprehensive, focused collection, no matter what the constraints. And once you consider yourself a collector, even in a modest way, then arranging your library in a sensible fashion will be easier to achieve, since your subject matter is targeted.

Kurt Thometz, proprietor of the Private Library, which consults on the organization of books, agrees that this specialized form of collecting is now the best way to go. Most other forms of rare book collecting are out of reach for the amateur (because of economics and availability), and modern fiction first editions, a popular subject, have lost their drawing power as more and more people collect them.

He has a final word for book collectors who are thinking of divesting: "Give your collections to a museum or library. Book dealers or auctions will give you a fraction of the value you will receive by donating

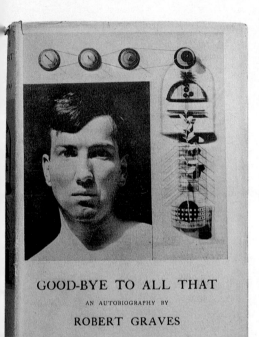

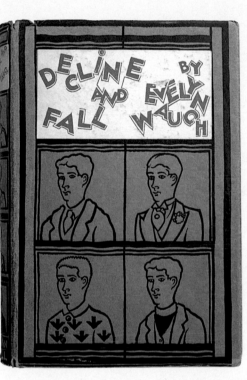

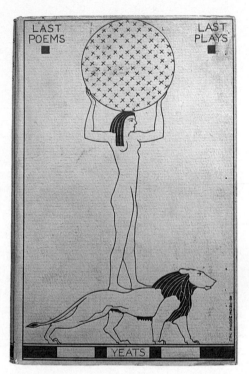

them. Most likely your taste is too personal for your heirs or relatives to share. Don't expect them to be interested in your African market literature, your early American bindings, your documentation of the Dada Movement, your carefully cultivated passion for the memoirs of pioneer Antarctic expedition leaders. Such collections are badly needed by the public archivists whose slashed budgets undermine their abilities to maintain and restore the wealth of information at their disposal. Today's collectors could be providing a great service to future generations as well as realizing their books' full value in the form of tax deduction."

Natalie Bauman urges collectors not to break up their illustrated books and sell them off as pic-tures, a practice she calls the democratization of books and prints. "People will take a great book and cut it—for instance, turn an atlas from the seven-teenth century into twenty-five maps, so that twenty-five people can now enjoy it hanging on their walls. It's tragic but inevitable."

Other collectors simply store their books in boxes and never put them on shelves. Such lack of appreciation recently led Stephen C. Blumberg, an acknowledged bibliomaniac, to resort to criminal activity. Over the last decade, he stole 21,000 books and manuscripts valued at an estimated $20 million from over 327 institutions in the United States, declaring their owners were indifferent to them. ✑

DESIGNER STACKS

Libraries Designed by Designers

ALL THAT MANKIND HAS DONE, THOUGHT, GAINED OR BEEN IS LYING AS IN MAGICAL PRESERVATION IN THE PAGES OF BOOKS. ∽

—THOMAS CARLYLE

MICHAEL GRAVES

ROBERT A. M. STERN

BILL BLASS

DAVID HICKS

JOAN VASS

JACK LENOR LARSEN

PAUL AND HERTA AMIR

"TEMPLIERS," A LIBRARY WALL FABRIC INSPIRED BY MEDIEVAL MANUSCRIPTS, DESIGNED BY DANIEL BEUGNON FOR BOUSSAC OF FRANCE, INC. ALSO USED FOR ENDPAPERS.

Michael Graves

"DESIGNING A LIBRARY IS ONE OF THE GRANDEST THINGS YOU CAN DO."

Michael Graves is more famous for buildings other than libraries. The Humana Building, the Portland Building, the Riverbend Music Center in Cincinnati, and perhaps most notorious of all, the Walt Disney Company Corporate Headquarters in Burbank, are stamped on the nation's consciousness as the work of a highly original mind. But his libraries are perhaps more greatly appreciated than any of these. The San Juan Capistrano Library in Southern California, the Clark County Library in Las Vegas, and the Denver Public Library speak of the humanity and love for books of this award-winning architect.

A professor at Princeton University since 1962, Michael Graves not only has daily contact with young people but is involved in education at all levels, having designed several cultural and educational buildings in many parts of the country. Graves has also designed furniture, furnishings, and artifacts—in particular, a range of bookends that confirms his place among the book people of the world.

"Designing a library is one of the grandest things you can do, perhaps because it's such an honored institution. I would much rather design a library than a bank or an insurance company. The library is a cultural center that reaches the heart of the urban condition. You can say that architects do not often get the opportunity to design churches—also a great calling. But church design tends to be a specialty, and local and congregational politics greatly limit the architect's freedom. Like designing a public school, it ought to be a great joy but frequently is not. People involved in libraries are usually superb, giving one every chance to do something good. If I had the choice, I would do libraries forever.

"In designing libraries, from major institutions to private residences, the challenge is to give a domestic feel to the space, whatever the size. The library at San Juan Capistrano, for instance, has something like twelve thousand square feet, so of course it is easier in a relatively small area to make cozy rooms, fireplaces, comfortable reading areas,

opposite

IN THIS DRAMATIC, AISLELIKE SPACE (A FORMER PORCH), THE SHELVING IS PAINTED FAUX BIRD'S-EYE MAPLE, THE LIGHTING IS ON A RHEOSTAT, AND THE DECORATIVE OBJECTS RELATE TO THE SUBJECT MATTER OF THE BOOKS—ART AND ARCHITECTURE.

and easy access to stacks. In an enormous city library like Denver's, on the other hand, which is more than four hundred and fifty thousand square feet, it is more difficult to achieve this feeling, and you have to be committed to designing small as well as large spaces for the people who go there. Imagine an eight- or ten-year-old child coming with classmates to a place this size as an introduction to the library. You want to create a place that won't overwhelm them and that they will want to use for the rest of their lives. So we tried from the beginning to make almost a library within a library, so that people feel they are alone with a book and not surrounded by a crowd of people. Your awareness of other people should not intrude on the relation between you, the book, and the setting.

"The best libraries allow you to come in and sense how they are used without people being there. In other words, the space is inhabited, and not a set piece.

"When we interview for a job like Denver, we contrast the traditional libraries from the Baroque to the Rococo with modern libraries, so many of which seem very icy. Who would want to read a book there? Don't forsake functionality, but give feeling to it. The use of wood and balconies give the great Bavarian and Austrian libraries warmth and intimacy. I spent a lot of time in the enormous library in the American Academy in Rome, designed by McKim, Mead, and White. It never felt enormous because it has shelves perpendicular to the walls, with reading spaces between them, in the style of earlier centuries.

"In the domestic context, space is often limited and the design therefore pragmatic. In other words,

we line the walls with shelves and then try to find a place where the owner can take out a book and read it. In my own case, I recently considered turning my living room into a reading room. I would then have library tables big enough to hold the volumes open that I frequently look at. Also I would add stack areas big enough to hold these large (mostly architectural and art) books. Then the room would become lined with books, together with artwork that I'm looking at or working with, and artifacts and furniture that I collect, giving them all more of a life. I've even thought of breaking through to the bedroom above and making that a balcony of books, but if I do that I need two more rooms, which at the moment I do not have.

"In my own library, unlike most architects who want to make a narrow space wider, I tried to make it seem narrower. The library is designed as a long aisle, lined on each side with shelves like minibuildings on a street. I left space both for books and objects—objects are good if they refer to the books in the library. I was fortunate to find a reading table for the room that was extraordinary in its functionality. It has flat drawers for prints and drawings and a tilted top like an easel. I would have liked to attach a ladder to the wall, but it would not work rolling across the rugs. Anyway, recently the library ladder has been overused decoratively.

"This year I gave my students at Princeton a library project to design. It was to be within a small town (Princeton), with theaters and other elements involved. When I gave them the site, one of the students came to me and said, 'I think it's particularly interesting that your site is across from the graveyard

THE BEDROOM IS OFTEN A PLACE TO PILE UP BOOKS THAT ARE
CURRENTLY BEING READ OR DISCARDED. THE WHITE CHAIR IS WHERE
MR. GRAVES SITS TO READ, HIS LAMP CONVENIENTLY IN PLACE.

above

MICHAEL GRAVES'S STUDY WITH ONE OF HIS FAVORITE PIECES OF
FURNITURE—A TILT-TOPPED READING TABLE WITH A BOOK OPEN
FOR HIM TO CONSULT.

opposite, top

MR. GRAVES ONCE SAW A COLLAPSIBLE BOOKEND DESIGNED IN THE 1910S AND COPIED THE IDEA, USING THE THEME OF ARCHITECTURAL FACADES.

below, left and right

WHEN THE ARCHITECT WORKED FOR DISNEY, HE CREATED AN AMUSING BOOKEND, CALLING ON MICKEY MOUSE TO SUPPORT THE BOOKS.

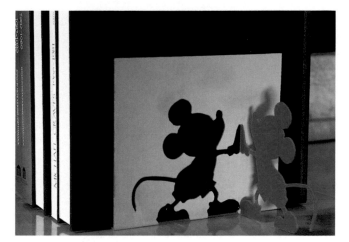

because of course the library will die almost immediately, probably within the century.' I asked him why, and he answered that since all texts would be computerized and all information electronically retrievable, books and libraries would be rendered obsolete. I suggested that when we started to record music, every composer doubtless said we would not need performances or live concerts anymore. The musicians would sit in a studio and we should all own recordings of everything and we could kiss Carnegie Hall good-bye. But these fears proved to be groundless. We have more live performances now than a hundred years ago, and people flock to the concert hall all the time. I should imagine that libraries made up with computer technology might make traditional libraries more valuable, in that they keep a different kind of record. Live publishing of some things is still better.

"When you look at an elevation or drawing or sketch done by an artist when engraving, for instance, was at its finest point of development, nothing can take the place of that experience—of seeing the authentic piece of work executed by the artist's hand.

On the other hand, while working on this library project with my Princeton students, certain precedents in library design were brought up for discussion, and I longed to be able to call up on the computer the plan of the city of Stockholm's round library, for instance, and resolve a dispute right there. Not that we couldn't go to the Marquand Library on campus and get the book, but there was an immediacy about the electronic alternative that would have helped clarify the discussion. Moreover, in the context of that precedent, there might have been a subtitle on the computer disk that offered all other libraries designed in a rotunda form, or indeed all other rotundas, information called up immediately in front of our eyes that could have further extended the debate. But this is a teaching tool. It would not threaten the importance of the original engraving. It serves different purposes. We have to keep other records, another kind of archive, in our libraries." ∾

Robert A. M. Stern

"PILES OF BOOKS IN CORNERS DO NOT OFFEND ME."

Robert A. M. Stern, architect to the rich and famous (Rockefellers, Rothschilds, and rock stars are his clients), reinventor of the shingle style of architecture, and master of a seventy-five-person architectural firm in New York City, has designed two libraries recently. One is in his small weekend house in East Hampton, New York, and the other is the Ohrstrom Library at St. Paul's School, Concord, New Hampshire. The two libraries are so extravagantly different that they perfectly encompass the sum of his thoughts and feelings about living with books.

"Architects who design houses get into trouble because of this century's big design battle between three understandable but, shall we say, contradictory client requests: 'I want big windows, to take advantage of the view, and have lots of light pouring in.' 'I collect art so I want plenty of space for pictures.' And third, 'I have lots of books and want enough bookshelves for them all.' Now if you add all three of these demands together, you realize you've run out of walls. So my job is to find a balance.

"I think perhaps people have too limited a view of where they can put books. They believe they have to be in a room specified as 'the library.' I think books can be anywhere in a house. Piles of books in corners do not offend me. Putting books in the dining room is a wonderful idea. My idea of heaven would be to dine, as well as to sleep, surrounded by books. When designing houses, we usually put books in the hall outside the guest bedrooms, because when you're a guest it's fun to browse through someone else's books (so much is revealed by their choices!) and if you've finished your own book and are stuck with nothing to read, you can just go out in the hall and pick out something.

"It's all a question of planning. I try to provide more spaces for books than my clients have books. That is wise for houses, and essential for libraries. Even though this is an age of computers and video, books, thank goodness, are going to be with us for a long time. To read a book is a very special experience—in no way duplicated in other media. We anticipate enormous growth of books at St. Paul's School,

for instance, where we recently designed the Ohrstrom
library. Happily St. Paul's, though beginning to
cruise along the electronic information highway, still
believes that books are fundamental to learning.

"My books are housed in two places. I keep
architecture books in the office, and the library is
deliberately placed in the center, so that as anyone on
the staff moves about, or when clients and visitors
come to see me, they pass through it. The architects
who work with me share my love for books. You will
see books piled on desks everywhere in our drafting
room. We use books in a very active way.

"In my bedroom in my East Hampton weekend
house, where I keep many of my other books, the
feeling of intimacy is achieved partly because of the
small space. But the books enhance that feeling. I
store in this room my future leisure-time reading and
those books I've actually read cover to cover. Books
you've read are like old friends. You look up and you
see a title that you've read and had pleasure from and
it makes you feel very comfortable.

"In my work, I always try to bring the intimate
scale of a residence to whatever I'm doing, whether it
be an office building or a school or whatever. On a
purely visual basis, books give an intimacy and personal dimension to a room such as no other decorative element can quite do. While the scale of the
library at St. Paul's is entirely different from that of
an office or a room in a house (Ohrstrom has space
for about a hundred thousand books), the feeling of
intimacy is there. Though geared for research, the
Ohrstrom Library is also in effect the living room for
the school. There is no student center on campus,
and the dormitories have very small lounge spaces, so

below left

IN STERN'S NEW YORK LOFT/OFFICE, AN INTERIOR ROOM, ACCESSIBLE TO THE WHOLE FLOOR, HOUSES A REFERENCE LIBRARY FOR THE ARCHITECTS.

below right

A BASKET OF BOOKS ON THE TERRACE OF ROBERT STERN'S SUMMER HOUSE INDICATES A FAVORITE READING PLACE.

the students tend to gravitate to the library in the evenings for their social encounters. You may go there and see students in the main reading room browsing through magazines. But also, throughout the rest of the building, you'll discover them holed up in deliciously cozy corners that provide a more intimate space for reading—and socializing.

"Too many libraries today are conceived of strictly in terms of efficiency, and built with emphasis only on information retrieval in a purely mechanistic sense, rather than on the experience of being with books, and understanding their relationship to each other and to you, the reader. But a library can and should be so much more than an information supermarket. The library is a community space, a place that invites personal interaction, involving other people sharing the experience of learning, of exchanging ideas, and of being lost in other worlds. A library should be a kind of club where one meets friends. For older people, the library is a social center, a place to overcome loneliness. For kids, it has that same function. You are with friends, sharing the experience of books and learning. What better goal could we have for the library in our time?" ☙

A BRONZE REPLICA OF THE PLACE VENDÔME OBELISK RISES FROM

AN EDWARDIAN TABLE ORNAMENTED WITH AN EIGHTEENTH-

CENTURY ARCHITECTURAL MODEL AND STACKED BOOKS. CUSTOM-

DESIGNED BRASS LAMPS ILLUMINATE THE BOOKS AND GREEK

HELMETS (SIXTH CENTURY B.C.) THAT BLASS DISPLAYS IN THE

BOOK WALLS THAT FACE HIS FAVORITE READING PLACE, HIS BED.

Bill Blass

"BOOKS ARE A PASSION FOR ME. BOOKS CHANGE PEOPLE'S LIVES."

When Bill Blass donated $10 million to the New York Public Library, a gift equaling the one given by Brooke Astor, Blass said: "You could consider it a miracle that I am in a position to do this! Books are a passion for me. Books change people's lives, and the New York Public Library is a civilized oasis in a chaotic city."

Creative head of Bill Blass Limited for more than four decades, the man described as "an icon of American style" has also been a trustee of the New York Public Library for close to ten years. Blass moves as easily in the world of books as he does in the world of fashion. His homes in New York and Connecticut reflect his close ties to the book establishment, a prized network of writer friends ("literary lions") and industry leaders ("corporate lions") who share his commitment to one of the seven great libraries of the world.

Recalling his earliest memory of reading and books, Blass says: "We had a place in the summer that had an accumulation of books that were not necessarily children's books. I read every one of the clas-

sics. Books at home belonged to fathers and grandfathers, but the public library was where you found books you wanted to read. At the height of the Depression a young person didn't own a lot of books. A library card was a passport to the outside world.

"My involvement with the library is no accident. I love books," Blass amplifies. "I read in the car. I read on airplanes. In town, even though I'm out every night I'll prop myself up in bed and read a chapter or two before I go to sleep. In the country, I read by the fire in a room I call my library simply because it has a large bookcase and adjoins a room devoted to the library furniture and accessories I've been collecting over the years."

The books in Blass's Sutton Place apartment and his eighteenth-century New Preston house range from current titles to medieval folios in Latin that Blass admits he can't read but was attracted to because of their extraordinary bindings.

"Although I buy most of my books for their aesthetic quality," Blass says, "they are in large part about subjects I'm interested in. The only books I

THE CITY

above left and top right

LEATHER-BOUND FOLIOS INTERMINGLE WITH EIGHTEENTH-CENTURY
GLOBES, ART ANTIQUITIES, AND SCULPTURE. THEY ARE THE
CENTERPIECES ON TABLES IN BOTH OF BLASS'S HOMES.

above right

A TROMPE L'OEIL SCULPTURE, POSITIONED BENEATH AN EIGHTEENTH-
CENTURY SIDE TABLE, SIMULATES THE BEAUTY OF A BOOK STACK.

have are those I'm reading or am waiting to read or
the books that chronicle the historical legacy of
houses, architecture, and decoration. I keep all my
books and magazines on fashion at the office."

Blass has also amassed a formidable collection of
twentieth-century literature, a treasure trove of autographed books given to him by his coterie of writer

friends. He's now safeguarding this growing collection in insulated boxes in the attic of his country
home, explaining, "Dampness is a problem in an
eighteenth-century stone house. It has destroyed
many of my books."

His home overlooking the East River is more
like the literary salon of a modern, urbane New

below

BOOKS GIVE WARMTH AND INTIMACY TO BLASS'S LIBRARY/DINING
ROOM. "I'VE ALWAYS FELT THE ROOM I HAD THE MOST BOOKS IN IS
THE PERFECT ROOM FOR DINING."

THE COUNTRY

above

BOOKS ARE ARRANGED AS ART OBJECTS ON A BOOKSTAND OF
VINTAGE BEAUTY. IT IS THE FOCAL POINT OF THE
BEDROOM/LIBRARY IN BLASS'S COUNTRY HOME.

top

AN INVETERATE COLLECTOR OF BEAUTIFUL THINGS, BLASS POSITIONS
A GRAND-SCALED IVORY-HANDLED MAGNIFYING GLASS BESIDE A
CLUSTER OF RARE BOOKS ON HIS REGENCY LIBRARY TABLE.

below left

COMFORTABLE CHAIRS "BOOKEND" A TABLE THAT HOLDS TITLES
FOR IMMEDIATE READING.

below right

IN BLASS'S CONNECTICUT RETREAT, COLLECTOR'S BOOKS ARE
DISPLAYED ON AN EIGHTEENTH-CENTURY DESK FRAMED BY HIS
CAMEO COLLECTION AND TWO PAINTINGS BY GOLTZIUS.

Yorker while his country residence resembles the
estate of an eighteenth-century English bibliophile.
Designed, in his words, as "spare settings for very
good things," both Blass homes register his signature
style. "I take the same approach in decorating my
home as I do in designing clothes. The objects we
surround ourselves with should make us feel special
and reinforce our sense of well-being. Rooms should
have more than one role." Blass's bedrooms are
designed to serve as library/sitting rooms. His dining
room in the city doubles as a library.

"I order books every week from the Madison
Avenue Book Shop and when I'm in London I go to
the same shop, Thomas Hendage, and hunt for
unusual books for myself or for friends. Last year I
found a beautiful four-volume collection on Russian
palaces and bought several sets of them. I kept one
and gave the others to people interested in Russian
decoration. I don't remember ever being given books
when I was young so it could be the reason I enjoy
giving them to friends today." ✑

RED-BOUND BOOKS HOUSED IN BUILT-IN PAINTED BOOKSHELVES

ANCHOR THE WALLS ON EACH SIDE OF THE FIREPLACE, OVER WHICH

HANGS A FAMILY PORTRAIT. TWO COMFORTABLE READING CHAIRS, A

VICTORIAN TURKISH RUG, AND FAVORITE OBJECTS ON THE MANTEL

ADD TO THE FEELING OF WARMTH AND INFORMALITY.

David Hicks

David Hicks, interior decorator and garden maker, has been one of the most influential designers of the twentieth century. His clean, subtly colored spatial palette, expressed also in his geometric carpet and fabric designs introduced in the 1950s, revolutionized postwar taste. In addition to having published over seven books himself, he is a passionate booklover and uses his visual talents in the most unusual way in designing his own library in his 150-year-old farmhouse in Oxfordshire, England.

"The idea of grouping together books with red bindings came to me after a visit to a beautiful house in Northamptonshire called Kelmarsh, belonging to the first Mrs. Ronald Tree, who became the well-known decorator Nancy Lancaster. All her red books were concentrated together. As a much younger man, I was also influenced by the library in the old royal palace in Venice, where the majority of books were covered in red damask or cerise silk velvet or red leather. Because of these experiences, I just fell in love with the idea of red books.

"So what I've done here is put all the red leather-bound ones together. I am binding a lot more, to add to them. But I also put all the ordinary books with red dust jackets together with them, so the effect is informal as well as very warm, especially in winter. The rest of the books are also color-coordinated, but less strictly. We have, for instance, my wife's paperback copies of Georgette Heyer's novels (romantic and very relaxing) mixed in with with cooler colors, black and brown, and some antique bindings.

"I haven't yet got all the blues and greens together. But I like a project that never ends, and a library is that. I suppose there are two to three thousand books here, as well as cupboards-full elsewhere in the house. A lot of them belonged to our grandparents, or were ours as children, and of course they ought to be edited out to make room for new ones. My wife is a great reader, and I'm a lover of books, so the library is always on the move. It never stops. It's a growing entity.

"That is what is pleasing about this library. I think there's something rather unattractive about a library that is completely formed with matching bindings in a short space of time. Those newly bound books are very hard to open, and there's something sterile about their chronological rigidity. I like the idea of a Victorian book next to Beardsley's *Yellow*

below left

A HICKS-DESIGNED LIBRARY LIGHT'S LAMPSHADE IS SLICED IN HALF
TO ILLUMINATE THE BOOKS AND NOT THE READER.

below center

A CUNNING CABINET THAT CONTAINS SHAVING KIT AND RAZOR
IS CONCEALED IN THE BOOKSHELF ABOVE THE WASHBASIN.

below right

DAVID HICKS DESIGNED THIS EBONIZED EGYPTIAN-STYLE BOOK
TABLE TO CONTAIN HIS OVERSIZE PERSONAL SCRAPBOOKS AND
DECORATING COLLECTIONS.

Book next to a completely modern book next to an antique calf binding.

"Upstairs, my bedroom library consists of all the white and string and cream-colored books that we possess, plus some antique ones that we inherited. Again, I thought, why not put all these together and it will create an interesting effect, and of course it does. I love waking up in this room looking out to the garden, the view framed by books.

"As for the design of a library, I think furniture or furnishings should never dominate the books. Yes, you must have two comfortable chairs, and good lighting is essential—not too much sunlight, which is bad for books. I like books on all four walls of a room whenever possible. That would not work of course in a very small space. I think the telephone and the fax machine are a part of modern libraries. I don't like the idea of home offices, but we can install these pieces of equipment in a library without them being noticeable. My fax machine is going to have a skirted table so it will be even less prominent.

"I remember Kenneth Clark's library in Hampstead (Lord Clark of *Civilization*). I think that was the first library I was enamored of. It was in an eighteenth-century house, and the library was full of the most wonderful books and objects. I said to myself then, I must do this one day. So here we are. It works well for me, this room." ✑

115

Joan Vass

"I'VE BEEN READING IN THE TUB SINCE I WAS NINE, AND MAY

EVEN DROWN SOMEDAY. WHAT A WONDERFUL WAY TO GO."

A learned German in an eighteenth-century spa had his Homer printed on rubber so he could read it in his bath," Joan Vass tells us, revealing that her favorite reading place is also the bathtub. "I've been reading in the tub since I was nine. I've dropped books in the water, wrecked many, and may even drown someday reading in the tub. What a wonderful way to go. I'm crazy about books. Even when I'm completely exhausted, I can't go to sleep without reading something first."

Art historian and ex-curator of the Museum of Modern Art in New York City, designer Joan Vass has a dual passion for books and art, both of which inspire the innovative clothes for men and women she designs. "I've learned whatever I know by reading and looking at painting, sculpture, and architecture."

Bibliophilia is evident in her book- and art-filled floor-through duplex apartment in the East 20s of Manhattan, a few doors away from her studio. Her home and atelier/showroom are oases in a neighborhood marked by Indian food stores and welfare hotels. "My intention in my work and my home is to rise above trends and to enter a world that lasts. Style lasts," Vass declares, as she delineates the elements that define her artistic and literary style of living.

Seemingly informal arrangements of books fill the old apothecary cabinets in Vass's library/sitting room. The core of her collection is arranged in carefully prescribed sections. "Fiction is over here, philosophy over there. Art history has its special place, as do my dictionaries. History and women's affairs, a book category that has grown enormously in the last several years, requires more and more shelf space. English literature is separated from American literature; short stories and novelettes from longer ones. Poetry has its own place, as do Italian and French lit-

opposite

BOOK-FILLED ROOMS DRAW YOU INTO VASS'S SPACIOUS DUPLEX
LOFT. A TROJAN HORSE MADE OF SCRAP WOOD BY GENE VASS ACTS
AS SENTRY. A BOOKSCAPE RISES FROM THE TABLE IN THE BEDROOM.

above right

TROMPE L'OEIL PILLOWS CELEBRATE THE BEAUTY OF BOOKS AND DECORATE A READING COUCH IN VASS'S LIBRARY.

below

BOOKS ARE EVERYWHERE, INCLUDING THE GREENHOUSE AND ROOFTOP GARDEN TO WHICH VASS FREQUENTLY RETREATS WITH HER CATS, REAL AND HANDCRAFTED.

erature. James Joyce is everywhere. Books on travel, music, and gardening have their own sections, as do the children's books I can't bear to give away."

Nestled in one corner of this room is the reading chair Vass's mother, another voracious reader, passed on to her along with books and furniture from their family library. "My parents had glass-fronted bookcases throughout the house that I wish I had today."

Vass reads everywhere and there is abundant evidence of this. Randomly piled books surround her bathtub and bed. A book door was built in her bedroom to camouflage a fire exit. Books topple tables and rise up off the floor in stacks that mirror the skyscraper view Vass can see from her favorite reading retreats: her bed and rooftop garden.

Vass buys books daily and scouts for them whenever she travels. New purchases can be glimpsed in bulging shopping bags. Compounding bookbag clutter are the volumes that she sets aside to give to her children, who are also collectors, or to donate to prison libraries, places people don't realize have a need for books.

"People shock me when they say they never read. When I was young, if people didn't read they would never admit it. Now, it's quite acceptable to be totally anti-intellectual," Vass laments. Her mood changes as she reaches for *The Best of Myles,* a spoof on book collecting written by Flann O'Brien. "He proposed a new profession, 'book handlers' who, for a price, could make books look as if their owners had lived, slept, and eaten with them. A book handler could be commissioned to go in and suitably maul a library for so much per shelf. As you can see," Vass laughs, "I wouldn't need one." ↝

above

BOOKS HOUSED IN RESTORED APOTHECARY CABINETS ARE
SURROUNDED BY PERSONALIZED ART ITEMS AND OBJECTS OF
COMFORT, LIKE A WOOD-BURNING STOVE.

JOAN VASS IN ONE OF HER FAVORITE READING CHAIRS. PORCELAIN
PEDESTALS HOLD "JUST READ" OR "SOON TO BE READ" VOLUMES.

COOKBOOKS AND BOOKS ON THE HISTORY OF FOOD AND DRINK
SHARE KITCHEN AND CLOSET SPACE WITH AN ARTIST'S COLLECTION
OF CHINA, POTTERY, AND WHIMSICAL KITCHENWARE.

Jack Lenor Larsen

"BOOKS, TO ME, ARE VERY STIMULATING SO I DON'T WANT

THEM IN DIRECT VIEW."

I don't like a room in which you are forced to sit and look at a wall of books. It was different when the leather bindings all matched and books were uniform in size. The architecture in those grand traditional libraries complemented and dominated the books. It is very different today," says Jack Lenor Larsen, renowned textile artist and environmental designer.

"They design modern book spines and book jackets for bookseller shelves and displays, not for home libraries. I find books visually distracting and intrusive. Unlike my literary friends who live in chaos with paper all over the floor, stacks of books and stuff everywhere, I am always trying to create tranquility. Books, to me, are very stimulating so I don't want them in direct view. I organize my books, and whenever possible their related collections, behind a movable wall of screens as I have in the city, or sheltered behind panels of parchment as they will be in the country. My books are viewable and accessible when I want them to be, but the room remains serene and open and accommodates my need for change. Even in the country where I have an under-the-eaves home office library, I have arranged my reference books on twenty-four-foot-long shelves, thirty feet high so they disappear when I am seated."

Described as a genius for reinventing space, Larsen creates innovative environments that "conceal and reveal." His space solutions work equally well in resolving how to store, arrange, and fit more books into less space. Larsen's library and its corresponding collection of art objects (he's a trustee of the American Craft Museum in New York City) are given "protective custody" behind reversible screens and double-faced panels of Larsen-designed fabrics. A modular system of adjustable cedar-and-glass shelves holds books on Bauhaus pottery, ancient crafts and textiles, contemporary graphics and design. Books on glass, silver,

opposite

A TRUSTEE OF THE AMERICAN CRAFTS MUSEUM, JACK LENOR
LARSEN HAS SURROUNDED HIMSELF WITH AN ECLECTIC
COLLECTION OF CRAFT AND FOLK OBJECTS IN THE
LIBRARY/GALLERY OF LONGHOUSE, HIS COUNTRY HOME.

THE CITY

above

**LARSEN'S LIBRARY AND ARCHIVAL COLLECTION OF ART OBJECTS
ARE SECRETED BEHIND MOVABLE SCREENS THAT WORK TO CONCEAL
AND REVEAL AS NEED AND MOOD DICTATE.**

BOOKS ON GLASS, SILVER, BASKETS, CERAMICS, AND ETHNOGRAPHIC
ART ARE PARALLELED BY GLASS-LIT SHELVES THAT EXHIBIT
RELATED COLLECTIONS IN LARSEN'S MANHATTAN LOFT.

LARSEN'S COLLECTION OF TEAPOTS FROM AROUND THE WORLD.

baskets, ceramics, and ethnographic art are bracketed by glass-lit shelves exhibiting related collections that Mr. Larsen has assembled in his global travels.

"When I was a child I had a fairy godmother who gave me a world map, a globe, an atlas, and a stamp collection and this could account for my fascination with far-flung places and my zest for collecting," he says. Larsen also recalls visiting a man, when he was young, who had an estate library that required four maids who would Vaseline his leather book bindings twice a year.

Jack Lenor Larsen's pragmatic views on living with books are vividly demonstrated whether you visit him in LongHouse, his sixteen-acre retreat in East Hampton, Long Island, or SquareHouse, the 2,000-square-foot "shoe box" loft he transformed into a habitat for Zen-style living in high-tension Manhattan.

"Books are light absorbing, and if I lined a room with them the space would become darker and

busier and the objects I enjoy taking off the shelves to focus on and arrange in the room would become less important. I think it would also be claustrophobic to walk a long corridor with books on both sides," he explains as he leads you from the entry corridor of his New York home into the living spaces at the opposite ends of the loft referred to as North Room and South Room.

"But when you position books on only one side they become easily accessible and it is satisfying to see volumes of books in passing. It makes walk-through space doubly useful," he adds.

"Most designers," Larsen observes, "arrange their books by size and color because they are concerned with the way a library looks best. But by the time you have several thousand volumes, as I have, it makes sense to organize books by subject or topic, writers or artists; size should be of secondary consideration. After a full week of having my books off the

THE COUNTRY

above

SPACE IS CARVED OUT OF LARSEN'S UNDER-THE-EAVES HOME
OFFICE TO MAKE BOOKS, MAGAZINES, AND OBJECTS NEEDED FOR
DESIGN RESEARCH ACCESSIBLE AND AESTHETICALLY PLEASING.

right

THE BOOK AS AN ART OBJECT, ONE OF A SERIES ON ANCIENT AND
TRIBAL ART BY EDMUND CARPENTER, DISPLAYED ON AN ORIENTAL
BOOK STAND AND PHOTOGRAPHED BY ADELAIDE DE MENIL.

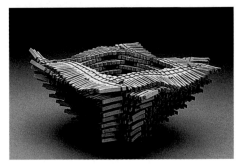

shelves for cleaning and reorganizing, this is the way I put them back on the shelves. It doesn't make them more beautiful, but all the more reason for my tenet of covering the whole with sliding panels."

A modular system of inch-thick shelves eight to fourteen inches deep, with vertical supports positioned at thirty-inch intervals, is recommended by Larsen to support the weight of books and prevent shelves from sagging. Glass shelves, he says, are strong, easy to light, clean, and inexpensive. You can get used plate glass for very little money and have the outer edge ground and polished.

Books should always be brought to the edge, he advises, and they are best arranged vertically. Recessed lighting not only helps when you're hunting for a book, it is also visually pleasing. When books are too big to fit on shelves, they can be placed on a window seat, a ledge, a platform, or a table large enough to take their weight.

Books on architecture, design, and textiles dominate SquareHouse in New York; books on gardens, gardening, landscaping, horticulture, and the history of eastern Long Island crowd the bookshelves of LongHouse, the seventh-century Shinto-inspired home Larsen designed in collaboration with architect Charles Forberg. Home base for the LongHouse Foundation Larsen founded, it is destined to become the first decorative arts museum on Long Island.

"The most valuable books in LongHouse," Larsen reveals, "were given to me by a neighbor, anthropologist Ted Carpenter. His gift of the seventeen-volume *Social Symbolism in Ancient and Tribal Art* illustrates the universal symbols that pre-literate people used to communicate with each other. It is a treasury of graphic beauty recording the passage of symbols from 'reverential' to 'referential.'

A reference library of several thousand books, chronicling the design, craft, and art heritage of people in China, India, and Japan are harbored in the design studio he walks to from his loft in Manhattan. ❧

Paul and Herta Amir

"A LIBRARY DESIGNED TO BE DYNAMIC."

In a newly built house in California, with natural daylight that pours in on a spectacular sculpture collection, where does the library fit in? For Paul and Herta Amir, who have over the years brought together a fine collection of sculpture, the requirements of the ground-floor library were very particular—the space must harmonize with and reflect the shapes and textures of the rest of the space.

For Arquitectonica, the Miami-based architectural firm, it was a pleasing challenge. "This was a library that combined books with art objects," says Laurinda Spear, one of the firm's founder-designers. "We wanted the feel of the room to be dynamic." This meant no rectangular floor-to-ceiling modules, but lines that float off the ground, and dramatic angles that create an almost sculptural quality to the shelving. (The only drawback to this meticulous geometric pattern—the shelves cannot be adjusted for height.)

The library bookcases were paneled and detailed in ebonized maple. The shelving was built around two right-angled walls. The smaller wall has bookshelves along one-third of its space, while the remaining two-thirds is paneled wood with ornamental wood detailing. Also inserted in this wall is a floating piece of granite at the center that opens up as a pass-through bar into the kitchen.

"This is a library for display and atmosphere, rather than for serious book retrieval," says Laurinda Spear. "Yet it provides a more intimate setting in which to read or talk to friends than the large living room, where all the sculpture is exhibited."

"We use the library a lot," Mrs. Amir agrees. "We have a space where we keep children's books for our grandchildren when they visit. My husband and I have a couch to ourselves for reading when we are alone." When the Amirs moved into the house, they had divested themselves of almost 80 percent of their

opposite

AT THE END OF THE BRIGHT, WHITE SCULPTURE-AND-LIGHT-FILLED

LIVING ROOM, THE LIBRARY GLOWS INVITINGLY.

above

THE FLOATING BOOK WALL CREATES A CORNER OF INTIMACY FOR

READING AND CONVERSATION.

A GRANITE COUNTER TO THE KITCHEN EMERGES FROM THE
PANELING, THROUGH WHICH AN ABSTRACT PAINTING CAN BE SEEN.

AUSTERE IN ANGLE AND COLOR, THE MASTER BEDROOM HAS ONE
WALL OF EXPECTANT BOOKSHELVES.

books, so they were starting afresh with this new library design. Now, Mrs. Amir says, the shelves are almost all full.

So are the bookshelves in the master bedroom where the dramatic angles of the downstairs library are repeated. (The unusually high bed board received its inspiration from the architectural design of some

of the windows in the house.) The Amirs have started to keep their oversize art books in this room, which, because of the size of the shelves, are stacked horizontally. "These are our most precious books, which we could never part with," she says. Now, while lying in bed, the Amirs can admire their treasures in comfort. ℀

Library Lighting

When people find it hard to read they blame their eyes and not their lighting system or how it's set up," says Peter Barna, lighting specialist and chairman of the industrial design department at New York's Pratt Institute. "I've seen people with the best lighting equipment put it in exactly the worst place. This occurs because what makes good lighting is not obvious, and the assumption that more is better is not necessarily true. Good lighting is a function of its location in the room, the amount of light actually coming from the source, and how it's distributed to the room and to the page."

Good lighting is a reading essential and the need for it only increases with age. For the normally sighted, it takes approximately twice as much light for the same task at fifty years old as it did when you were twenty. But how can you determine the optimum lighting arrangement? The Illuminating Engineering Society, Joseph Ceterski of the Lighting Research Center at Rensselaer Polytechnic Institute, and Pratt's Peter Barna told us how.

Choosing the Right Amount of Light

The amount of light people need to read comfortably depends on their own visual abilities, age, and the material (quality of paper, size of type) they're reading. It is recommended that when you plan your lighting, make your decision based on the most demanding text you're likely to encounter. The Illuminating Engineering Society recommends that you provide lighting adequate for reading "type smaller than that on a newspaper and handwriting in pencil."

While there are standards as to how much light is required for certain materials, if you have flexible fixtures you can easily adjust the light level for each situation. "I think we change our lighting depending on what and how we're reading," Peter Barna says. "If I'm reading a report or editing I'll use a light directly over the material, which I don't necessarily do when I'm reading for pleasure."

The light on the book you're reading should be brighter than your surroundings, but should not contrast sharply with the ambient light. There should be a "coziness" between the book and the reading light. Too high a contrast between the brightest and darkest areas of your room can cause visual discomfort. To check if your light contrasts are too stark, glance back and forth between the lightest and darkest objects in the room. If your eyes are having trouble adjusting to the contrasts, increase the light levels in the room. This will allow you to read comfortably while still maintaining pockets of brighter areas for visual interest.

Selecting the Right Fixtures

"People primarily choose lighting because of how it looks as an object, a decoration, and that's how lighting is sold, as a piece of sculpture," Peter Barna explains. "Really, the first thing to consider is not how a fixture looks but how well it performs. How much light does it give and how is it distributed in the room? In a lighting store, with a hundred or so fixtures going, it's very difficult to determine this, even if you know what to look for. Many people end up choosing lighting that's too strong for their home and that produces a lot of glare."

There are two types of glare: *discomfort glare* and *disability glare*. Both reduce the ability to read well. Discomfort glare, the type of glare produced by the headlights of an oncoming automobile, is easily identifiable and corrected because it causes people immediate and recognizable discomfort. But disability glare, which reduces the ability to see well but does not cause immediate discomfort (though it often leads to eyestrain, fatigue, and headaches), is harder to identify and fix. "It's like bad posture,"

Barna says. "You don't notice it until you start having lower back problems."

The best way to determine if your current lighting situation is producing disability glare is to take a glossy magazine and sit where you normally read. If you notice any "veiling reflections," reflections of objects on the page that make it difficult to read, move yourself and/or the fixtures until the reflections are eliminated or reduced to a more comfortable reading level.

The next thing to consider after function is the *energy efficiency* of your system and the effect you want to create. Depending on your budget and/or ecological concerns, this will figure differently in your decision. The type of bulb you choose—incandescent, quartz, or fluorescent—will have a direct effect on the efficiency of your system and the overall mood of your library.

Fluorescent bulbs are the most energy efficient of the three and come in warmer and cooler color tones. Cooler-toned fluorescents are usually preferred if the lights are used primarily during the day, and warmer-toned fluorescents when used mainly at night. Fluorescent lighting was originally designed and used in office settings, but a whole new breed of compact fixtures are finding their way into the residential market because of their energy-saving qualities.

Quartz ranks second in terms of energy efficiency. The bulbs can cost five to six times that of fluorescents or incandescents, but they also have a longer life span. Quartz tends to be a preferred lighting source for daytime reading because of its cooler tone. It also works well aesthetically in libraries of a more modern design. The problem with quartz is that because the bulb is compact, designers tend to create fixtures that produce highly concentrated light that is not conducive to long-term reading.

Incandescent bulbs are the least energy efficient, but they produce a softer lighting effect that makes them popular with nighttime readers. They are also the least damaging to books.

No matter which source or combination of sources you opt for, it's best to choose fixtures that can be easily adjusted to be kind to your eyes and to fit reading needs and mood.

Using Light as a Decorative Element

Lighting dictates not just how well you see, but *what* you see. It can be used not just as a necessary tool, but to create and enhance your library environment as well. Lighting conveys a certain mood or atmosphere. Shelf lighting can draw attention to cherished objects and volumes; track lights can highlight certain areas of your room.

Peter Barna describes the approach he took to lighting design for the Folger Shakespeare Library in Washington, D.C. "We used a painting by Kissman called *Passing of the Storm* as a metaphor for the quality of light we wanted. It's a beautiful painting of that moment on the water when the storm has just passed and the air is fresh and there are still clouds on the horizon, but it's not overly bright. It was a moment of transition and expectation that we were after, so we didn't light the underside of the ceiling vault. We left it as it was, like clouds that were just breaking."

In general, high contrasts of light and dark within a room will produce tension and drama, whereas overall soft lighting and pastel colors create a mood of relaxation. However, either one of these treatments carried to extremes can be boring. If you choose the more soothing option, make sure you will have enough light. If you opt for the dramatic option, which calls for more focused concentrations of light, make sure your room is lit enough to handle it.

To maintain these dramatic differentials, disguise

the sources that are giving most of the light, thereby making the light from the sources that are visible appear greater than it actually is. "It's what they do in a nice, intimate restaurant," Barna explains. "You want people to believe it's the candles on the tables lighting the space, even though it isn't."

Arranging *overhead lights* at right angles to your stacks will illuminate all shelves well, even the lowest ones. There are also recessed ceiling fixtures designed to gently wash over shelves, and adjustable track lighting systems, which can be used to aim light directly at your bookshelves. Wall-mounted and standing lamps can work very well. Fixtures known as "strip lighting" that clip directly onto book-holding units may be appropriate for books you want to high-light—but they may also give the effect of store display cases and should be used with caution. Bill Blass's use of custom-made brass lamps flexed over wall-to-wall bookcases is a good example of how lighting can enhance a room without overpowering it.

Since all light damages, the amount of time you actually focus lighting directly on books or objects should be limited. For perfectionists, the general rule that many museums go by is low light (five footcandles) eight hours a day over a course of five days. (Normal office lighting is usually fifty to seventy-five footcandles.) Of course, if you use your shelf lighting less often you can increase the intensity.

The traditional library lamp, often placed in the middle of the desk immediately in front of the reader, is not a good choice. In general, standing and table lamps should be placed either directly over your left or right shoulder or slightly behind you. This keeps distracting brightness from entering your visual field and reduces veiling reflections caused by glare.

When reading in a favored chair next to a table lamp, make sure the lamp is placed so the lower edge of the shade or cover is not materially above or below eye height. This will prevent discomfort from peripheral brightness. If you're using a floor lamp, make sure the shade is no higher than eye level. If the lampshade height is above eye level, position it close to the right or left rear corner of the chair for reading comfort.

Small *high-intensity reading lamps,* popularly used to read in bed, do not sustain long periods of reading and can lead to eye strain. A better choice would be a more evenly lit room with lighting equipment placed so that you can read in a comfortable position with no shadows cast on the page. An eye shade is recommended for bedtime companions who do not share your interest in late-night reading.

Overhead lighting should never be positioned directly above reading or work surfaces, like desks or tables. Reading furniture should not be positioned directly under overhead fixtures. The greater the amount of light cast on the task from immediately above, the greater the loss in visibility. In general, the more diffuse the light from the fixture, whether wall-mounted, standing, or table lamp, the less the glare. Choosing matte finishes for library walls and reading furniture, rather than gloss finishes, will further reduce glare.

Natural light, filtered in through skylights and windows, while psychologically satisfying, can also lead to glare and reading discomfort. It is also more damaging to books than all three artificial light choices. While drawing the blinds will eliminate this problem, sitting parallel to or away from unshaded windows will reduce glare and still allow you to enjoy the benefits of a sunlit library. To reduce the likelihood of damage, position books so they are not exposed to direct sunlight (though some conservationists hold that indirect light is equally as bad) and draw the blinds when the room is not in use. ❧

The Art of the Bookshelf

The shape of the bookshelf, like that of the bed, has not changed much since it was first designed. When books were larger (medieval Bibles, for instance), shelves were bigger. When paperbacks were invented, shelves could be small and light. Today there are basically two forms, built-in and freestanding. Built-in shelving acts as a decorative feature with moldings, spaces for fireplace or television, architectural details reflecting elements in the room, and so on. Freestanding bookshelves are adaptable to almost any space but are more limited in their visual appeal.

According to Joe Moccia, designer for The Shelf House in New York, most built-in units are made of solid woods like mahogany, cherry, maple, and oak. "The wood should be dry and stable so as to avoid warping." Shelving 1 inch thick, 36 inches long, and $10\frac{1}{2}$ inches deep accommodates most books. If the shelf is to be longer, the thickness should be increased to $1\frac{1}{8}$ or $1\frac{1}{4}$ inches to prevent sagging. Freestanding units are generally held in place by aluminum tension poles attached at the ceiling and floor with rubber pads, the shelves leaning against the wall for extra support. With a $\frac{3}{4}$-inch shelf, poles should be spaced a maximum of 31 inches apart, considering the load of the books. If the shelf is 1 inch thick, the poles can be spread farther apart.

Variations on these basic concepts are legion. Étagères, pyramid shapes, ornamental wire poles, and revolving stands are all useful ways of housing books. Units such as Gothic niches, Palladian frames, and tapering towers have also been created to add interest to a book collection. Floor-to-ceiling bookcases functioning like paneling or elaborate wallpaper are favorites of architects and designers. Bookcases as room dividers, as architectural elements, as space makers, are often brought into a room layout.

Designer Jack Dunbar created a floating book wall on a geometric grid, that is, eight individual boxes two feet long and two inches thick, with perforations on the sides so the shelves can be adjusted. The boxes are joined by removable columns. Jack and Judith Dunbar painted these bookcases with an automotive paint that has enormous impact resistance and allows the books to slide in and out easily. For a brilliantly inexpensive book wall made out of another kind of box, a young architect and his wife salvaged white plastic milk crates left for pickup outside a neighborhood supermarket. Stacking them up, they created an instant faux Louise Nevelson wall-to-wall, floor-to-ceiling library.

Perhaps the most advanced experiment in bookshelves came from the Columbia University classroom of architect Frederick J. Kiesler forty years ago. The ultimate bookcase would be curved like a halfmoon, with the user in the middle, able to reach with his outstretched arm every book on the shelves. As the user accumulated more books, the arc would be extended to full circle.

Today, we are beginning to have to accommodate a new inhabitant in the library—the computer. As we move into the next century, we can no longer consider only book storage in our reading rooms, but also the computer, disks, and other paraphernalia that go along with the electronic library. With so much

A FREESTANDING PIECE OF FURNITURE SERVES AS A HANDSOME BOOKSHELF.

information now being put on CD-ROM, and so many readers browsing the Internet and other online services, book rooms without space for a computer screen, keyboard, and boxes of disks will be as inadequate for tomorrow's booklover as a dog kennel for an elephant.

Probably the most often seen mistake in the installation of bookshelves is the failure to factor in the sag quotient. How heavy are your books? Are you going to include your old records (they are much heavier than books)? Do you have oversize volumes? The answers to these questions will greatly affect the thickness and spacing of the shelves. One other vital question most of us forget: Will there be room for more books (and disks), which you will undoubtedly acquire? Perhaps, as Linn Cary Mehta, wife of writer Ved Mehta, commented, "The best bookshelf is an empty one—room for more books." ℰↄ

WALL-TO-WALL
BOOKS

The Well-Stocked Library

BIBLIOMANIAC IS ONE

TO WHOM BOOKS ARE LIKE

BOTTLES OF WHISKEY

TO THE INEBRIATE, TO WHOM ANYTHING

THAT IS BETWEEN COVERS HAS AN INTOX-

ICATING SAVOR. ✑

—SIR HUGH WALPOLE

STANLEY BARROWS

NICOLAS BARKER

BARBARA KIRSHENBLATT-GIMBLETT

KENNETH JAY LANE

NIALL SMITH

Stanley Barrows

"I ALWAYS ASK FOR BOOKS FOR CHRISTMAS."

Some libraries are more than just book rooms. They tell a life story. Such is the case with Stanley Barrows, whose wide-ranging and erudite career was emblazoned on the walls of his apartment like an illuminated manuscript.

Born into a highly educated, religious family (both his grandfather and father were Episcopal ministers), Mr. Barrows grew up surrounded by books. Yet the written word was not his first love. "I became interested in design and decoration at an early age. I did stage sets at school and at college." Discouraged from finding work in this field at the end of the Depression, he went to the Parsons School of Design instead, and ended up as director of the European studies program there.

Europe played an essential role in his life. He went to Paris first as a Parsons student in 1939, and through the school's connections, was able to look at museums, private collections, and the great palaces of France and Italy, learning for the first time to appreciate the contribution made to art by the European patrons of the Renaissance and after. In 1945 he returned to Europe, this time stationed with the Air Force Engineering Corps at Caserta, afterward staying at a study center in Florence. From this trip he brought back hs first pieces of Italian furniture.

"I had started to collect French books in Paris," he recalled, "particularly those on French design and architecture." Later his library grew into one of the finest decorative arts collections in the country, with early eighteenth-century architectural books and an early edition of Palladio among other rare volumes. Inspired by this treasure trove of design literature, Mr. Barrows became one of the preeminent teachers of interior design in this country, first at Parsons, and from 1968 until 1985 as chairman of the design department at the Fashion Institute of Technology. He remained active as a consultant until his death in

opposite

WHEN WALL SPACE IS A PROBLEM, A WELL-KNOWN SOLUTION IN HISTORIC AS WELL AS MODERN HOUSES IS TO HANG PAINTINGS IN FRONT OF BOOKSHELVES.

below

THE BEDROOM/LIBRARY DISPLAYS ART, BOOKS, AND PERSONAL
TREASURES IN COLORFUL HARMONY.

1995. His students, who praised his insistence on visual harmony and good proportions, include many of America's top decorators, such as Tom Britt, Mario Buatta, Albert Hadley, Edward Zajac, and Richard Callahan.

During most of these years Stanley Barrows owned two apartments, his home and a smaller one he used as a study. Later he relinquished the study and managed to find space for all his books, paintings, and work materials together, truly a challenge. It meant transforming the bedroom into a second

library, and adding additional bookshelves in the hall and living room. Collecting design books is always problematic, for many of them are oversize or are printed in portfolio form. Mr. Barrows designed specially high and deep shelving to house these works. The most striking piece of furniture in his living room, however, was not a chair or a table but a book cabinet of boulle marquetry dating from the the Regency period, which he found at an auction.

For lack of space—and for visual variety—Mr. Barrows hung paintings right over some of the books,

below

IN THE LIVING ROOM TO THE LEFT OF THE BOULLE CABINET, EXTRA-
DEEP HORIZONTAL SHELVING CONTAINS RARE ART PORTFOLIOS.

a familiar sight in many English country houses. Altogether, there were at least five thousand volumes in this modest space. "The whole apartment is designed for my books," he said. "I know where everything is. I don't read much fiction," he added. "Edith Wharton, of course, because of her interest in design. I own books by her collaborator, Ogden Codman. I found a copy of Beatrix Farrand's book recently."

More frequently, Mr. Barrows reread his books. "I never feel you've understood Proust until you've read it three or four times." Sometimes suffering from insomnia, he read a lot in bed. "I always have at least three books ready to read into the night."

Experiencing the warm colors of his rooms, the fine bindings and overscale editions that fill his bookshelves, the paintings by former students, the eighteenth- and nineteenth-century English and European pictures and plates, and the elegantly positioned porcelain and statuary, we discover a man who was steeped in the decorative arts and who used his well-traveled eye to create a enlightened, cultivated universe for those he welcomed here. ᏬᎧ

Nicolas Barker

"WHEN PEOPLE ASK ME, 'DO YOU COLLECT BOOKS?'

I ALWAYS SAY, 'NO. BOOKS COLLECT ME.'"

Nicolas Barker is perhaps the quintessential book person. Surrounded by books of all shapes, ages, and sizes, he has a faintly nineteenth-century air of bookishness. Scholarly, dry, witty, he has spent his life surrounded by the printed page. Growing up as a Cambridge University professor's son among fifteen thousand books "dotted about the house," his playpen was the Cambridge University Press, where he first became enamored of printing, so much so that his father bought him his own printing press.

"Like Toad messing about with boats, I have messed about with books ever since I can remember. I was what they call a voracious reader, a three-book-a-day child. The printed word has a magnetic attraction to me. A seven-week-old newspaper, even the telephone book, is good enough for an obsessive reader like me."

It was natural for the young Barker to move from reading to the sensual apparatus of books themselves. "Some books have physical properties which make them the right form in which to read.

I don't mean necessarily first editions—though of course it is desperately moving to read Keats in the first edition."

Mr. Barker started his career in publishing in the production department of Rupert Hart-Davis, ending up in charge of their book design and production—"the engine room," as he calls it. In 1965 he did the same for Macmillan ("wonderful historic experience—nothing had been altered since the nineteenth century") before moving to the Oxford University Press. In 1976 he was called by the British Library to become their first Head of Conservation.

"The British Library is the most used library in the world," Nicolas Barker says. "But the problem with books is that unlike other rare objects, they aren't simply looked at and admired, they are handled on a daily basis. A clockmaker, for instance, is normally in the business of making a clock *go*. But in the preservation department of a museum, a clockmaker responsible for a clock made by Leonardo da Vinci and decorated with jewelry by Benvenuto Cellini preserves it by stopping the clock and making a facsimile

opposite

THIS MAGNIFICENT CARVED BOOKSHELF WAS, ACCORDING TO ITS OWNER, "THE CHEAPEST SHELVING YOU COULD BUY IN 1898 WHEN MY FATHER GOT MARRIED."

above

THE GROUND FLOOR OF NICOLAS BARKER'S WEST LONDON HOUSE
SERVES AS BOTH LIBRARY AND STUDY. NEW AND OLD BOOKS PILE UP
ON SOFAS AND CARPETING AS SHELVES PROCLAIM NO VACANCY.

below left

EVEN THE "LOO" SERVES AS BOOK STORAGE, AS WELL AS
ENTERTAINMENT FOR VISITORS.

below center

NICOLAS BARKER'S FIVE CHILDREN WERE INTRODUCED TO BOOKS
EARLY, THEIR FAVORITES WITHIN EASY REACH AT BEDTIME.

below right

ALL THE WAY UP THE SEVERAL STAIRCASES, BOOKS LINE THE WALLS.
WHAT WILL HAPPEN WHEN THEY REACH THE ROOF?

for people to examine. As a book conservationist, on the other hand, I had fifteen million clocks and they all had to *go*—that is, function for people to read!"

Over the next sixteen years this quest involved devising methods for preserving heavily damaged manuscripts as well as laying the foundations of a chemical process, graft polymerization, to strengthen the leaves of books in bulk. "It works in the laboratory. All it needs is one of the great chemical industries to have the vision and the capital to build a plant to treat books by the thousand."

He has now retired from the British Library, and is advising the National Trust on the libraries in its properties throughout Britain. "There are about 150 of them, large and small. Some, like the great libraries at Blickling Hall, are huge, among the most important historic libraries of the country. Others are quite small—the early library of a Cornish parson, Hannibal Gamon, preserved at Lanhydrock, for instance, or the yeoman farmer's library at Town End in the Lake District."

As for his own library in London, it is, well, idiosyncratic. "Gordon Ray, the great American book collector and head of the Guggenheim Foundation for many years, came to visit me here once, I remember. I had to leave him for a while to attend to my five small children and when I came back, he straightened up from looking at the books and said, 'You'll have to do a lot of talking before you can convince me that there is any order or method in this collection.'"

Order or method may not be the guiding principle behind Mr. Barker's library. But affection certainly is. "I tend to regard my collection as a kind of foundling hospital for books, books that need a home. Booksellers give me books when they simply cannot sell them, because the books are hopelessly imperfect or damaged. I'm not in the least bit interested in perfect books. I'm interested in the fact that it has lost one-tenth of its leaves. How did it lose them and why? It's all part of their history." Mr. Barker looks around at his stuffed shelves, lined with his happy patients, and smiles. "I open my arms very wide for books to take refuge here," he says. You can almost hear them rustling in gratitude. ❧

above

BURIED IN BOOKS! DESPITE THE MAYHEM IN BARBARA'S LIBRARY,

THERE IS "METHOD TO THE MADNESS." THE SALVAGED CARRELS,

CARTS, TABLES, AND BOXES ON WHEELS, SEEN IN THE FOREGROUND,

HOLD THE BOOKS SHE RETRIEVES FOR WORK-IN-PROGRESS

PROJECTS. HER FORMIDABLE RESEARCH LIBRARY LINES THE WALLS

THAT SURROUND HER.

Barbara Kirshenblatt-Gimblett

"Books have always upstaged everything in my home."

She calls herself "curator of the common-place," but Barbara Kirshenblatt-Gimblett's home library is anything but. It is more reminiscent of the secondhand bookstores that once lined the streets of Lower Manhattan than the home of a professor of performance studies at New York University and her husband, artist Max Gimblett.

"I am whatever I am teaching, writing, or involved in," Barbara explains. Her library reveals her career as anthropologist, folklorist, writer, scholar, curator, and specialist in Yiddish studies and culture as well as her devotion to cooking and food.

Books overwhelm the "found space" (forty-five hundred square feet) Barbara and Max rescued on the Bowery—an appropriate location for the salvaged books, bookcases, book tables, bookstands, book trolleys, book carts, and reading-room furnishings they foraged. Hidden within a nondescript building and guarded by a metal plate door, access to their home is achieved by ringing a bell and getting a welcoming nod from Max, who looks out of his studio two stories above a restaurant supply store.

A freight elevator or steps that bear the marks of a hundred years of stair climbing bring you to an endless corridor of books that rise from what was once a factory floor to an eleven-foot arched ceiling. Nestled in the corner is a neatly made bed that also serves as a resting place for bundles of books. They've been tagged for disposition, as have the boxes and stacks of books that surround the bed and line the hallway.

Upon entering the library/living room you're enveloped by a landscape of fifteen thousand books. "Books have always upstaged everything in my home," Barbara says. "When I lived in a small house in Texas my furniture was my books. It took an enormous U-Haul to move them all to New York."

The east wall of the library/living space houses the core of her cookbook collection. Wooden shelves sag under the weight of books in fourteen languages that record the historical, multicultural appetite of the world.

"Nobody collects cookbooks as indiscriminately as I do. I contact women's organizations, scout book fairs, visit museum bookshops, put ads in newspapers, and ask friends to be on the lookout for me." The most extraordinary cookbooks in Barbara's "safe house" for books are a near-complete set of the *Settlement House Cookbooks* and nineteenth- and twentieth-century cookbooks written in German, Hungarian, French, Hebrew, Polish, Spanish, and Yiddish—many of which languages Barbara can read and speak. She is especially moved by reprints of the seventeenth- and eighteenth-century cookbooks she

discovered, some of them in manuscript form and handwritten by women.

"I began by choosing one of the smallest categories available in food literature, Yiddish cookbooks. Then, as I had more income, I collected German, Polish, Russian, Lithuanian, and Ukrainian cookbooks because of their related cuisines. The Middle and Far Eastern cookbooks came later on and they track Indian, Persian, Tibetan, and Afghan foods I experienced in my travels. Food to me is not just recipes, it's the social and cultural history of people."

Among the books Barbara prizes the most is the first cookbook she got when she was ten. "I am touched by reading a recipe; I visualize what the final dish will look and taste like. I sight-read recipes like people sight-read music.

"It's really hard for me to draw the line between the books I collect because of my lifelong interest in them and those I need in my reference library. Currently, I'm writing a social history of Jewish cook-

books, so I need material no library can provide."

Barbara's reference library dominates the remaining cavernous space. Floor-to-ceiling steel shelves house books on museums, world's fairs, and amusement parks needed for her course on tourist productions. Books on theater, dance, and rituals are organized for her courses in performance studies. Books on decorative art, design, and photography are accessible for the course she developed on the aesthetics of everyday life.

Barbara says that if she were to do it all over again she would opt for freestanding mobile book stacks, lining them up perpendicular to the wall. She recalls an apartment that had book walls on tracks so they were easy to move around. "Stacks on wheels could be set up to create the working rows you need for concentrated research." Barbara is accomplishing this now with a secondhand restaurant serving wagon and a new library cart. "I wheel my book carts over to my computer so I have all of the material I need close at hand. They also work as holding pens for books that need to go back on the shelves when a project is complete."

Three computers are jammed into a book wall, and Barbara demonstrates how she uses them to retrieve information from what she calls "that great library in the sky. Although I do adore books, access to electronic books offers pleasure of another kind. You don't have the sensual enjoyment of holding a book in your hands, the tactile pleasure of paper and binding, but there is great satisfaction in being able to move through an electronic text, access material, and add to it as well. No, you can't go to bed with a floppy disk, but I've done it with my laptop." ∾

IN THE DINING AREA OF THE KIRSHENBLATT-GIMBLETT HOME, MINIATURE FOOD UTENSILS FROM CHINA, AFRICA, MEXICO, HOLLAND, AND BELGIUM ARE GROUPED IN STILL-LIFE VIGNETTES ABOVE A CAREFULLY ARRANGED UNITED NATIONS ASSEMBLY OF COOKBOOKS.

COOKBOOKS CROWD THE SHELVES OF BARBARA'S OPEN KITCHEN. THEY SURROUND A FOOD COUNTER, STOVE, AND AN UNSEEN DINING TABLE AND ROCKING CHAIR BARBARA RETREATS TO WHEN SHE'S NOT WRITING OR DOING RESEARCH.

Kenneth Jay Lane

"I GREW UP AS A READER. IT NEVER ENDS."

Kenneth Jay Lane makes jewelry, but he also runs a twentieth-century salon out of his luxuriously appointed apartment in New York City. Writers, musicians, and artists flock to this palace for parties, with the urbane host, like a benign wizard, overseeing the entertainment. What gives his apartment such a civilized air is the number of books it contains. There are books everywhere—on the floor, in the air (the living room's sixteen-foot ceiling has a balcony stuffed with books), and in elegantly proportioned shelves.

"There were two huge doorways opposite each other," Mr. Lane explains. "I saw the opportunity to frame them with bookshelves. I closed in one doorway so that bookshelves go all the way up. The other remains a door."

But his book collection overflows the shelving built into the walls. He keeps books on the floor, the piles getting bigger as his housekeeper piles more on top. "I get sent a lot of books," Mr. Lane explains. "Many friends of mine are writers." Bruce Chatwin, Gita Mehta, Joan Collins, Brad Gooch—the names are eclectic, and the books keep coming. "I also love nineteenth-century literature, biography, fiction."

Along with his books, Mr. Lane has a fine collection of nineteenth-century Orientalist art. He has books on that subject, too. "I don't know where they are," he sighs. He tries to keep English biography together, books on India together, travel books together. But he runs out of space and the new ones get put under chairs. "I try to recycle," he says. "I give current novels away when I have read them."

He is planning to build more bookshelves. Sometime. If he can find any wall space left. Meanwhile, the books pile up. ⌘

opposite

THE GLOWING COLORS OF KENNETH JAY LANE'S ORIENTALIST ART

COLLECTION REFLECT THE BRIGHT MODERN DUST JACKETS OF THE

BOOKS WAITING TO BE READ BESIDE THE SOFA.

above

NIALL UNWINDS WITH A BOOK AND A CUP OF TEA IN HIS READING

LOCATION OF CHOICE. A BOOKSCAPE SURROUNDS HIS BIEDERMEIER

DAYBED AND KEEPS BOOKS WITHIN ARM'S REACH.

Niall Smith

"BOOKS GIVE A ROOM A PERSONAL STAMP."

Books are the only thing that give a home personality and humanity," Niall Smith, antique dealer and Biedermeier specialist, says. "You can put out all the tchotchkes you like, but they won't reveal anything about you. Books give a room a personal stamp."

Experienced in the art of decor, Niall transformed a cavernous space in what was once a machine-shop building into a resplendent home for himself and his books. An extensive section of Irish and American classics and an amazing series of books on early American history starting with the year 1000 reveal his literary interests. A first edition of Hall's book on Ireland, the assembled work of Booth Tarkington, *The American Spirit in Letters and Art*, *The Makers of a New Nation*, *The Lure of the Frontier*, and *The Winning of Freedom* are visible amid his finely bound volumes.

This Irish-born antiquarian opted for an unconventional habitat, part refuge and part archive, to make room for his growing collection of books and Biedermeier furniture. "I had to have a loft because I couldn't bear selling anything," Niall says, admitting he eventually opened two shops to absorb the overflow.

Open the door of Niall's home and you discover a gallery surrounded by a book wall he had handcrafted and then painted himself in Biedermeier style. Niall designed this modular room divider to complement Biedermeier cabinets, chairs, and tables of rare provenance and to provide an expandable system for his collection of books.

"I wanted to keep the look of the loft intact, sprinklers and all, as a refreshing reminder of the twentieth century and as a direct contrast to what I've put in it," Niall explains, adding, "I couldn't take the book walls up to the ceiling because of the building codes, but they work well just the same." In addition to separating his library/drawing room from dining and sleeping areas, Niall's book wall creates an environment conducive to "the last private act, reading."

Reading is Niall's declared at-home pastime, with biographies, novels, and novellas his books of choice. "I didn't grow up with a TV and still don't have one today. When I'm home I read stretched out

above

A BIEDERMEIER FRUITWOOD SECRETAIRE DOUBLES AS A HOLDER
FOR BOOKS AND EXEMPLIFIES NIALL'S PREFERENCE FOR FURNITURE
THAT CAN SHELTER AND EXHIBIT BEAUTIFULLY BOUND VOLUMES.

right

A BIRCH BIEDERMEIER CABINET (BERLIN, 1820) ACQUIRED BY NIALL
SMITH FOR HIS COLLECTION OF MICRO-MOSAICS.

on a couch," he says, as he gestures toward a side table he calls his lectern. "I prop up a book here and read for hours."

Niall has very strong ideas about how he arranges his bookshelves. "I'm very particular about how I keep my books," he admits. "I only like books flushed to the front of the shelves. I hate when they're recessed. I arrange my books by subject, not author. I'm not a very organized person, but I do have a fair idea of where everything is."

Towering stacks of magazines and superscale books surround couches and chairs and bear testament to Niall's claim of never having thrown a book away. "Occasionally I'll get rid of some of the magazines, but never books. I'm also very fussy about getting books back when I do lend them. My mother, Birdie, wouldn't even let a book out of the house. Anyone who wanted to read one of her books had to come to her house and read it there."

Niall is always on the lookout for pieces of furniture that can also shelter the beautifully bound volumes he's collected. "Now that I'm running out of room I'm thinking of replacing the two vitrines in the dining room with some Biedermeier bookcases I found, after much searching." ๛

below

TOWERING STACKS OF MAGAZINES AND SUPERSCALED BOOKS
SURROUND COUCHES AND CHAIRS AND BEAR TESTAMENT TO NIALL'S
CLAIM OF NEVER HAVING THROWN A BOOK AWAY.

Bookplates

above and opposite

A FEW OF THE MAGNIFICENT BOOKPLATES FROM MARGO MULHOLLAND'S COLLECTION.

The youngster who scrawls his name in the front of his book is no different from the booklover who uses a printed, illustrative and personal bookplate," states the introduction to a catalog from one of the best sources for bookplates, Ex Libris in New York. "Although this mark of ownership was originally intended to safeguard against loss (and still does), bookplates have evolved over centuries into sophisticated and personal statements with great appeal for all. Ex Libris, the Latin for 'From the library of . . .' is extensively used, and has come to be universally understood as an alternative name for a bookplate."

The history of the bookplate can be traced to fifteenth-century Germany with the birth of movable type. As printed books were rare and highly valued, bookplates became a unique, picturesque way to identify ownership. Roger Rosenblatt, essayist and editor, pondered this use of the bookplate in his performance piece *Bibliomania*. He rhetorically asked: "Should we not abjure our pettiness, open our libraries, and let our most valued possessions fly from house to house, sharing the wealth. Certain clerics with vows of poverty did this. Inside their books was printed not EX LIBRIS but AD USUM—for the use of—indicating that it is better to lend than to keep, that all life's gifts are transitory."

Bookplates have been a book and library accessory that have drawn the talents and interest of many famous artists and public figures. Notable artists and engravers of the bookplate include Albrecht Dürer, Paul Revere, Aubrey Beardsley, Marc Chagall, Kate Greenaway, Rockwell Kent, and Leonard Baskin. Patrons of the bookplate include George Washington, William Penn, Franklin Roosevelt, Jack London, and William Randolph Hearst. Major universities, like Harvard, also have had bookplates designed for special collections.

Ex Libris—Anita Loos

While bookplate prices vary, depending on the skill and popularity of the artist, with some designs in the $1,000 and over range, the usual cost is between $100 and $500. "You don't have to be a millionaire to commission a bookplate," says James Keenan, a Boston collector who compiled the directory *American Artists of the Bookplate: 1970–1990.*

Collectors can find bookplate artists by viewing examples of their work in society newsletters, exhibitions, public and university libraries, illustrated books, or a directory such as Keenan's. In addition, the American Society of Bookplate Collectors and Designers publishes a quarterly newsletter that also facilitates contact between collectors and artists. ∾

Gertrud Laesecke.

Bookbinders and Conservationists

Bookbinders are really book doctors, tending to patients that have become damaged by water, fire, or other elements, dried out, or in some way simply worn out. Bookbinders and conservationists restore cloth and paper bindings, rebind leather bindings, retaining as much of the original binding as possible, reback and reattach boards to

right

TALAS OFFERS A COMPREHENSIVE "FIRST AID KIT" FOR BOOKS. BASED ON RECOMMENDATIONS FROM CAROLYN HORTON'S *CLEANING AND PRESERVING BINDINGS AND RELATED MATERIALS*, THE KIT IS IDEAL FOR BOOKLOVERS AND BOOK COLLECTORS ALIKE. IT CONTAINS A STARTING SUPPLY OF MATERIALS FOR BOOK REPAIR AND CARE, INCLUDING A ONE-WIPE DUST CLOTH, MAGIC RUB ERASER, SCALPEL BLADES, LEATHER PROTECTORS, BOOK-SAFE GLUES AND PASTE WITH APPLICATORS, MENDING TISSUES AND LINEN THREAD, SEWING AND KNITTING NEEDLES, ALONG WITH SEVERAL BASIC COLOR DYES FOR COVER TOUCH-UPS. IN THE BACKGROUND ARE ENDPAPERS DESIGNED BY DIANE MAURER.

leather volumes, deacidify book pages, machine tool
or hand tool on leather, construct protective cases,
and in every way nurture a sick book back to health.

"The aim of conservation is not to make a
favorite volume appear new again," conservationist
and binder Jerilyn Glenn Davis explains, "but to preserve it as a historic artifact." When a binder perfects
a book to the point where it is unrecognizable, he or
she changes its nature and diminishes not just its mon-
etary value, but its human and social value as well.

Wilton Wiggins and Douglas Lee have a studio
in Santa Fe where they look after books sent to them
from all over the world. "We'll take an old book
that is badly warped, for instance. We will flatten it
and make a protective case to house the book once
the work has been done." Customers vary in their
demands, their books having sentimental value to
them. "Sometimes they will spend $200 to $300 to
repair a book they may have paid $50 for."

There are several places in the country that spe-
cialize in book restoration. One of the most famous
is Talas, in New York City, which provides every kind
of book repair material for the booklover. Elaine
Haas, founder of Talas (and labeled the best-known
secret in the book business), describes her company
as "a flea market" offering a wide assortment of
goods. For instance, Talas provides a solution called

"THE BIBLE BELT"—COMMERCIALLY PRINTED BIBLE ON A LEATHER BELT, WITH GOLD-PLATED BUCKLE, BY NORA LIGORANO AND MARSHALL REESE.

above

AN OLD "CLAMSHELL" PRESS, WITH A FLY WHEEL, DISK TO DISTRIBUTE INK, AND HAND-FED PAPER, IS POWERED BY A FOOT PUMP LIKE A BICYCLE.

Wei T'O that neutralizes acid (one of the major destroyers of paper). Fortunately, according to Haas, publishers have begun to produce a large number of their titles on acid-free paper.

Another important development in book-making is do-it-yourself book binding. For example, at the Center for Book Arts in New York, founded by Richard Minsky, you may learn the art of printing and book binding and bind your own books, choosing the colors, materials, and shapes that will best contain your favorite stories or poems. "For centuries, knowledge of the craft associated with book-making was passed from generation to generation by way of a rigid system of apprenticeship," wrote Brian Hannon in an introduction to "Masters of the Craft," a recent exhibition at the Center for Book Arts. Today, people can take courses for themselves and discover the joy in printing and binding, an experience that not only produces a beautiful object at the end, but also affirms the power of the unbroken chain linking us to the history of the book.

For names and addresses of bookbinders and conservationists, see the Resource Directory. ❧

left

MOST TYPE CASES HAVE DRAWERS
LIKE THIS ONE, FILLED WITH PIECES
OF METAL TYPE THAT MAKE UP THE
WORDS IN A BOOK.

above

MAUREEN CUMMINS, BOOKMAKER
AND TEACHER AT THE CENTER FOR
BOOK ARTS IN NEW YORK, SITTING AT
HER TYPE CASE.

LITERARY LAIRS

Writers' Libraries

 MUST STUDY POLITICS
AND WAR, THAT MY SONS
MAY HAVE LIBERTY TO
STUDY MATHEMATICS AND PHILOSOPHY,
GEOGRAPHY, NATURAL HISTORY AND NAVAL
ARCHITECTURE, NAVIGATION, COMMERCE,
AND AGRICULTURE, IN ORDER TO GIVE THEIR
CHILDREN A RIGHT TO STUDY PAINTING,
POETRY, MUSIC, ARCHITECTURE, STATUARY,
TAPESTRY, AND PORCELAIN. ∾

—JOHN QUINCY ADAMS

A CLOSE-UP OF "TEMPLIERS," THE LIBRARY WALL FABRIC DESIGNED
BY DANIEL BEUGNON FOR BOUSSAC OF FRANCE, INC. (SEE
ENDPAPERS AND PAGE 94).

JEAN STEIN

RICHARD HOWARD

JOHN RICHARDSON

FRANCES FITZGERALD

CHARLES RYSKAMP

THE READING SOCIETY
LIBRARY IN CORFU

SIR FITZROY MACLEAN

ROGER ROSENBLATT

Jean Stein

"A GATHERING PLACE FOR ARTISTS AND WRITERS."

Every home needs a room that's soothing and removed, a kind of oasis from the rest of the world. In Jean Stein's Upper West Side apartment, that room is the library, with its pleated, fabric-covered walls, its overflowing bookshelves, where you might find inscribed copies of William Faulkner's *A Fable* and Jessica Mitford's *Hons and Rebels* ("To Jean, fellow-rebel"), its overstuffed sofa, and its subtle lighting—so secluded that you can sit there without anyone else in the apartment aware of your presence. There are two entrances, as in a drawing room farce.

In 1989, Ben Sonnenberg asked Jean to take over the publication of *Grand Street,* and for two years the magazine was run from a small room just across the hall from the library. Betsey Osborne, who was assistant editor, remembers that that also had its farcical side: the little room held four people (sometimes five or more on those occasions when the full staff was assembled), two computers, bookcases, file cabinets, a fax machine, a copier, a grand piano (which had been

ensconced there long before the magazine moved in), and a staggering quantity of manuscripts to be read and mulled over. Jean would shuttle back and forth between this office, the sunny dining room, and the library, where she met with authors and literary agents and contributing editors and friends.

Sitting in the dusky library takes awhile before you notice the Joseph Cornell box on the mantelpiece or the Giacomettis—a painting of his mother, drawings of Jean—on the wall. Edward Said might be there, discussing an article for *Grand Street,* or Kenzaburo Oe might stop by to meet young American writers, or Dennis Hopper and Norman Mailer, or Joan Didion and John Gregory Dunne. Walter Hopps, the magazine's art editor, might fly in from the Menil Collection in Houston, Texas, inevitably pacing up and down, filled with an inexhaustible flow of ideas, punctuating them with gestures from his ever-present cigarette, while Jean sits—*perches*, really—on the huge, plush sofa, nibbling on Parmesan cheese and walnuts and sipping

below

SOME OF JEAN STEIN'S FIRST EDITIONS, GIFTS FROM ARTISTS,

BOOKS BY FRIENDS.

ginger ale. Or a dozen Czech writers might arrive, along with William T. Vollmann, somehow looking more Eastern European than any of them.

The library overlooks Central Park, and on days when the street isn't being repaired, Jean opens the French doors and lets the fresh scent of the park come wafting in. One early-morning meeting came to a sudden halt when a long line of elephants, each one tightly clutching the tail of its predecessor, emerged from among the trees. Everyone clustered around the window to watch them amble calmly southward toward Madison Square Garden and out of sight, then settled back to their conversation as if nothing unusual had happened. In *that* room, nothing is truly surprising. ∾

Richard Howard

"I REALLY WANTED TO BE A READER, NOT A WRITER."

There is something both austere and luxurious about this space. It expresses the owner's one fixation: books. But the books are everywhere—uncountable, unquantifiable, prodigal in their number, shape, size. Richard Howard is a poet and a translator, and his home is his library. He lives, eats, and sleeps in his library. His whole apartment is his library. His life and his work are all in plain view on the walls of his bibliomanic nest.

"I know where to find them all," says the poet calmly. "They are kept alphabetically. But I have no idea how many there are."

Richard Howard started reading early, but was not interested in writing until much later. "I liked the idea of reading; in fact I really wanted to be a reader, not a writer." Both sets of grandparents were readers and book collectors, so Mr. Howard learned early the appeal of a fine binding. He does not collect books for that reason, however. His books serve his work. "I am constantly using books from these shelves," he says. "Of course, I occasionally try to have a purge. I also have a drive toward editions—that is, a series

of books published in one volume. But it is hard to part with a book."

Some of the books on the shelves (which he built himself) come from his grandparents. Others are his own. He has published many volumes of poetry, and many more books in translation from the French, including works of Cocteau, Genet, Barthes, Foucault, Mauriac, and Beckett. Many of their books adorn his shelves in the original language.

Mr. Howard learned French as a child, very fast, on a car journey he took with his family from Cleveland to Miami Beach. Much later, when he began work on the translation of De Gaulle's memoirs, the general commented on his excellent French and asked him how he had learned it. To the general's consternation, Howard replied that he had learned it in a car in five days.

He won a Pulitzer Prize for poetry, but it is his translations that have earned him almost greater respect. As writer and critic Richard Bernstein says, Richard Howard is "among the most skillful practitioners of a craft often considered best performed

**RICHARD HOWARD AND MAUD ENJOY A GOOD BOOK AT THE
POET'S DESK.**

when it is least noticed." Mr. Howard is currently embarked on the mammoth task of translating Proust's *A la Recherche du Temps Perdu*. The old translation of that title, with which we are familiar, is "Remembrance of Things Past." Mr. Howard's new and more accurate title is "In Search of Lost Time."

He sees translation as a constantly fluctuating art. "The master work, the generating text, contains multiple possibilities," he explains. "The translator can only choose one, and the one he chooses is going to show signs, after thirty years, of chips and cracks." Thus great foreign masterpieces often require a new translation to retain the work's freshness for a new generation of audiences.

The poet lives part of the year in Texas, where he teaches writing at the University of Houston. How does he solve the problem of having books in two places? "I sometimes miss a book that is in the other place," he concedes. "But I love institutional libraries. I used to think I was in competition with public libraries and that I was winning. But now I prefer them to my own. You know you will get what you want at any of the great university or public libraries of the world."

Richard Howard has lived in his New York apartment for fifteen years. He shares it with his dog, Maud, also an avid reader. "I wanted to live in a tree house," he says, "to feel enclosed. Yet I like to travel a lot, and with an apartment like this, it is easy to make one's escape. I can put my dog under my arm and leave without a backward glance." ❧

below

THIS IS THE APARTMENT OF SOMEONE WHO GOES TO BED AT NIGHT,
WAKES UP IN THE MORNING, AND MAKES HIS EXITS AND HIS
ENTRANCES WITH BOOKS.

John Richardson

"I'D LIKE TO HAVE EVERY BOOK ON PICASSO EVER WRITTEN."

Where writers write has always intrigued people. Freezing garrets, rented rooms, mountain cabins, have all contributed to the mythology of the making of literary masterpieces. Few writers, however, have been able to create such an elegant temple to their craft as John Richardson, whose neoclassical library in Connecticut has become home.

The library was built originally as a getaway place for him to write, undisturbed, his four-volume biography of Picasso. Mr. Richardson's main house is designed with a series of interconnecting rooms circulating around a central hall—a charming idea, but hopeless if you want to avoid guests or work without interruption. The surrounding land offered a perfect spot for privacy, on top of a small hill, looking down through trees and shrubs to the swimming pool below.

The design of the library was the brainchild of Cuban-born architect Ernesto Buch, who responded to John Richardson's fond memories of his schooldays at Stowe. The little temples and pavilions designed by Sir John Vanbrugh, William Kent, and Capability Brown that decorate the English boarding school's parkland are recalled in the colonnaded facade of Mr. Richardson's library and the interior details of pediments, columns, statuary, and moldings.

The impressiveness of this building might daunt some authors, but its lack of pretension, comfortable furnishings, and warm colors have so seduced Mr. Richardson that he has just about moved in for good. "I originally thought I would simply walk over here every morning and write," he says. "What has happened is that I live, eat, and sleep here nearly all the time." With its tiny kitchen and sleeping alcove, this room is the ultimate example of living with books and the ideal space for a committed writer, whose massive project on Picasso looms ahead for years to come.

Not that writing was John Richardson's first love. "I wouldn't have dared to think of being a writer," he confessed one afternoon, taking a break from the word processor and sitting by his pool. "Maurice Richardson, my first cousin and thirty years older, was the writer in the family. My grandmother wrote children's books. No, I thought I was going to be a painter. At Stowe I painted and did collages all the time."

opposite

BOOKS ARE STACKED ON THE FLOOR IN FRONT OF A LONG TABLE HOLDING A COLLECTION OF IMARI PORCELAIN.

top

A LOUIS XIV ÉTAGÈRE SERVES AS A BOOK CARREL IN THIS
WRITER'S PARADISE.

above

JOHN RICHARDSON, TAKING A BREAK FROM THE CURRENT
VOLUME OF HIS BIOGRAPHY OF PICASSO, LOOKS OUTSIDE
TO THE DORIC PORTICO LEADING TO HIS GARDEN.

Mr. Richardson pursued his studies in France, and then enrolled in the Slade School of Art in London. When World War II broke out, the school was evacuated to Oxford and John Richardson was given digs with a professor of premedieval history, whose library the young art student pillaged. Shortly afterward, deserting art, he started writing short pieces for magazines on art and ballet, progressing to fiction criticism, which meant he was sent practically every new novel published—a fine way to start a library. "I had precious tastes," he allowed. "Eighty books by the Sitwell family, complete sets of authors, that sort of thing." He never had room to store his books, leaving them with his mother and friends. Until one friend died, leaving John's books in the hands of a rogue who sold them all.

The next phase of John Richardson's life, 1949 to 1962, belonged in Provence with the art collector and aesthete Douglas Cooper, with whom Richardson helped put together one of the finest modern collections of Cubist art. Douglas Cooper had a superb library, the main part of which, on his death, was bought by the Getty Museum in Malibu. Richardson's books merged with what was left of Cooper's, forming the nucleus of the library he has today.

Finally, Mr. Richardson came to the United States, originally as representative for Christie's, then as a writer and critic. His library expanded in every direction—architecture, art, decorative arts, twentieth-century literature, auction catalogs. . . . "Since working on Picasso, my library has become even bigger," he sighs. "I'd like to have every book on Picasso every written. I also collect every Xerox and fax on the subject. Picasso covered so many topics—

below

THE LIBRARY IS DOMINATED BY PILASTERS, CORNICES, AND
ARCHITECTURAL DETAILING IN THE NEOCLASSICAL STYLE, PULLED
TOGETHER BY THE GLOWING BLUE-GREEN GLAZED WALLS.

Surrealism, Spanish politics, poetry, mysticism, the cultural and social history of the twentieth century. That's a lot of books."

In spite of the size of his library, he would never unload. "I worry about space, but I can't get rid of a book. They are all over the place, on chairs, on the floor, even in the car." Does he ever feel overwhelmed by his books? "I wouldn't mind that feeling," he says. "I've just inherited the library of a friend—a collection of books on the arts and the applied arts. At the moment they are in the garage in boxes. But I could never turn away a book. Never." ❧

Frances FitzGerald

"How to merge two lifetimes of books?"

They say you can learn a lot about people by looking into their medicine cabinets. Books are equally revealing. For Frances FitzGerald, Pulitzer Prize-winning author and journalist, her books are like a resumé of her career. "I write about Asia, thus I have a collection of books on Asia. I am currently working on a book about American politics in the Reagan era, so I have accumulated many books on that subject. I have a collection of books on religion as a result of my book on American religious groups. Many of my friends are writers, so I have their books, too."

For most of her writing life, she has lived and worked in an apartment overlooking the East River in Manhattan. Her living room is her workroom and library. Originally, bookshelves took up wall space on each side of the fireplace and on the east wall, but a suggestion volunteered by her friend Mark Hampton, for whom libraries are something of a specialty, caused her to wrap the north wall also

in books, "instantly transforming the look of the room," in the words of the grateful owner.

The books are arranged alphabetically by subject matter—books on the Far East to the right of the mirror, poetry and literature in the corner, and so on. On the whole she can easily find what she is looking for. "I also use the Public Library, and the library at New York University."

Recently, however, she married the *Wall Street Journal* correspondent James Sterba, and having decided that their apartments were too small for both, they found a larger apartment for their life together. This meant facing what many new couples dread as much as dealing with in-laws—how to merge two lifetimes of books? Marriages have faltered on this issue. "There is no room for my books!" the resentful cry goes up, as though the books were children.

In FitzGerald's case, rescue was close at hand. She has kept her old apartment (which is within walking distance of the new one) as a work space, so

opposite

THE ARCHITECTURAL DETAILING ON MARK HAMPTON'S TWELVE-FOOT-HIGH BOOKCASE MATCHES THE DETAILING OVER THE LIVING ROOM DOORWAY OF THE NEW APARTMENT.

below

FRANCES FITZGERALD CALLS THIS HER "PURGATORY" TABLE, ON WHICH BOOKS SENT TO HER BY HER PUBLISHER AWAIT THEIR FATE— TO BE READ OR DISMISSED. AROUND THE BUDDHA'S NECK IS A "LITERARY LIONS" AWARD FROM THE NEW YORK PUBLIC LIBRARY.

many of the books simply stayed there. Jim Sterba has a study in the new apartment, where most of his books are now housed. The only merger was of his and her books on China, Vietnam, and Central Asia, subjects about which both have written extensively, and a smaller combination of twentieth-century fiction by the fireplace.

The big merger took place in a splendid bookcase designed specially by Mark Hampton to fit the new apartment. "That was the only area on which I asked advice," Frances FitzGerald admitted. "Our new living room has sixteen-foot ceilings, and the question was, how far should the bookshelves go up the wall? Build them all the way up, and they might give the impression of tilting. Built low, they might look out of proportion." After consultation, the bookshelves were built twelve feet high. That is high enough to require a ladder, but as she says, "We have read most of those books anyway, so rarely need to reach them."

She reads compulsively, mostly but not exclusively books related to her work. She makes a definitive break when her workday is over. "I am always reading a novel, or non-work-related nonfiction, for contrast and relaxation, and for when I go to bed. You don't want to go to bed with work." As well as reading books, Ms. FitzGerald reads *The New York Times* every day, cover to cover. "I miss a lot of wonderful articles in other papers such as *The Wall Street Journal,*" she says in a tactful reference to Sterba's employer, "but I simply do not have time to read more

than one." She devours magazines, which are mostly kept on a bench in the kitchen of her old apartment. "I read articles, but not fiction or poetry. Somehow to read a story or poem in a magazine diminishes the work. You feel it is disposable, like the magazine in which it appears. A book is better, more permanent."

For many journalists, particularly those involved in current affairs, the rapidly expanding electronic technology of database retrieval is very appealing. While Frances FitzGerald recognizes the usefulness of instant accessibility to reference materials, she does not see this as heralding the end of the book. She attributes to editor Aaron Asher the observation that "the book is the most efficient retrieval system we have." Anyway, she adds, "you can't take a floppy disk to bed." &

AFTER THE FAR WALL WAS SHELVED IN WITH BOOKS, THE ROOM IN
FRANCES FITZGERALD'S ORIGINAL APARTMENT CAME TOGETHER AS
A MORE HARMONIOUS WHOLE.

AN ENGLISH EIGHTEENTH-CENTURY GLASS-FRONTED BOOKCASE

CONTAINS BOOKS ON ENGLISH ART (OVERSIZE ON THE BOTTOM SHELF),

INCLUDING WILLIAM BLAKE'S WORKS ILLUSTRATED BY THE AUTHOR.

Charles Ryskamp

"I LIVE WITH ONE OF THE BEST ART-HISTORICAL

LIBRARIES IN THE WORLD."

Charles Ryskamp's father was a professor, three of his uncles were professors, and the house in Grand Rapids, Michigan, where he grew up had two book rooms, one upstairs and one down. In this environment of bibliophiles, the young Charles started acquiring his own books before he was ten, buying them, sticking file folder labels in them as bookplates, writing his name in them, and numbering them.

It was also a natural progression for Charles Ryskamp to become a scholar himself, teaching English literature at Princeton University, before moving on to run two major literary and artistic institutions, the Pierpont Morgan Library (where he was director from 1969 to 1987) and The Frick Collection, where he is currently director. "During my teaching years, I had an office at Princeton which accumulated more and more books," he says. "At the Morgan, the director's office at the time was two stories high, filled with the most glorious books, none of which, alas, was my own. Now at the Frick I live with one of the best art-historical libraries in the world."

When we talk about books, he says, we must also talk about where to sit down and read them. "I'm a great believer in desks. I have desks everywhere, in the hall, in my bedroom, two in my living room in Princeton. The English have always understood this so well; every guest room in an English country house has a desk for reading and writing." In the libraries in his apartment in New York and his house in Princeton, both furnished with desks, books and drawings compete for space along with porcelains and objets d'art. Yet there is a strong sense of discipline in the arrangement of his rooms. Given the number of books and the relatively small space of his libraries, how did Mr. Ryskamp avoid the sense of oppression that so many crowded libraries seem to produce?

"I worried about how I would manage," he concedes. "Particularly when I was moving jobs and living quarters. I kept books in three places. Many of my literary and history books remained in my office (available to my graduate students) and at home in Princeton. I moved to New York all my books on English art and a considerable number of those on other aspects of art history."

Thus he knows where everything is. But the key to his success at organization is that Mr. Ryskamp, as well as being a passionate booklover, is also an editor at heart. Unlike some obsessive collectors, he prefers to unload some of his volumes when necessary. "I have given large numbers of books to Princeton and many special volumes to the Morgan. To move them

IN HIS NEW YORK APARTMENT, PROVING HIS BELIEF THAT BOOKS
SHOULD BE ACCESSIBLE AT ANY TIME OF DAY OR NIGHT, HE DINES
AMONG HIS BOOKS.

all was impossible, so I kept only those I actively used."

For scholars who constantly consult their books, it is vital that the books they need be instantly accessible and not quarantined behind locked doors or in glass cases. "I had bought a drawing from a famous seventeenth-century collection," Mr. Ryskamp recalls, "in which all of the several thousand drawings had remained anonymous. Lying in bed at three o'clock in the morning, I suddenly was struck by an inspiration as to the identity of the artist. I leapt out of bed, stark naked, and rushed to my library, where in my collection of art books I found the one which contained proof that I was right. Even though the Frick has some of the greatest art history books ever assembled, I would never have been able to enjoy the immediacy of satisfying my hunch there."

Mr. Ryskamp continues to buy—and to pare down. He admits, though, that if he changed jobs or moved he would have to make another radical adjustment. That worries him less than the familiar complaint of book people—where to stack the books that do not obviously fit any category. "It is the miscellaneous works that defeat me," he explains. "For instance, last weekend at my house in Princeton, I was determined to find *The Earls of Creation* by James Lees-Milne, a marvelous book about the eighteenth-century English patrons of houses, gardens, and architecture. Could I find it? No. That's the kind of book that slips through."

So in this case, like every other mortal reader frustrated by such a fate, he was reduced to buying a new paperback copy. ❧

below

IN HIS LIBRARY IN PRINCETON, NEW JERSEY, CHARLES RYSKAMP
MIXES SCHOLARLY BOOKS ON ART AND LITERATURE WITH HIS
PICTURES AND PORCELAIN COLLECTION.

The Reading Society Library in Corfu

The Reading Society: A quiet place in Greece

Perhaps the civilization that has most profitably passed down its heritage to us through books and reading is Greece. It is not surprising, therefore, that one of the most civilized small libraries to be found anywhere in the world is on a remote island off the mainland of Greece. Called The Reading Society, it was founded on the island of Corfu in 1836 by the philosopher and scholar Peter Brailas-Armenis, and is the oldest literary society of its kind in Greece. It is housed in a yellow-painted building that stands high up in the town, almost opposite the Palace of St. Michael and St. George. The Reading Society contains an impressive library of literary and historical works, and includes a unique collection of manuscripts, engravings, paintings, and maps related to the Ionian Islands.

Philosophy, literally meaning "love of wisdom," was invented by the ancient Greeks. From the sixth to the fourth centuries B.C., Greek rationalists worked out a complex system of thought concerning the nature of the universe and humans' place within it, asking questions that are as pertinent today as they were all those years ago. Their theories of morality, expediency, religion, and materialism, written down in their histories, dialogues, and plays, gave us a body of work that we still consult as though written in the language of our own century. Politics, democracy, history, tragedy—these are words that the ancient Greeks created, and that have lived in the human heart for over two thousand years.

"Wonders are many on earth, and the greatest of these are humans," Sophocles wrote. Wonders such as this glorious library confirm the ancient Greeks' belief in the human mind and its ability to attain knowledge and, through knowledge, to achieve joy. ↩

opposite

INVITING AND COZY, THIS LIBRARY IS OPEN TO ANY VISITOR WHO MAKES AN APPOINTMENT.

above right

VOLUMES OF GREEK HISTORY AND TOPOGRAPHY LINE THE SHELVES OF THIS HOUSE OF KNOWLEDGE IN CORFU.

Sir Fitzroy Maclean

"I FIND MY BOOKS BY INSTINCT."

This is the library of Sir Fitzroy Maclean, war hero, traveler, author, and farmer. His life story could be the subject matter of a contemporary thriller. Before the outbreak of World War II, Sir Fitzroy was in the Diplomatic Service, with postings in Paris and Moscow. During this time, he traveled extensively in the remote regions of Central Asia, penetrating as far as Chinese Turkestan and Afghanistan.

During the Second World War, Sir Fitzroy served in the first Allied parachute unit to operate in the Middle East. In 1943, at the age of thirty-two, he was secretly dropped by parachute in German-occupied Yugoslavia as Winston Churchill's personal representative and commander of the British Military Mission to the Yugoslav Partisans. He remained in Yugoslavia until 1945, all enemy attempts to capture him being unsuccessful.

Throughout the war, Sir Fitzroy also found time to be a member of Parliament and served in the Churchill and Eden governments as Undersecretary of State for War. A fluent Russian-speaker, he has since then spent many years negotiating cultural and other agreements between Britain and the former Soviet Union.

But Sir Fitzroy is more than just a practical man. He happens also to be a writer, and has turned his adventures into a series of books, among them *Eastern Approaches, Take Nine Spies, The Isles of the Sea, Bonnie Prince Charlie,* and *A Concise History of Scotland.* He wrote an account of the famous state trial of Bukharin and Rykov, as well as many television programs.

That is why his library in Strachur House, Argyll, Scotland, is so vivid—it represents a pictorial history of Sir Fitzroy's colorful life. "The books here are partly inherited and partly collected by me over the last seventy-five years," he says. "I read them either for pleasure or because I am working on them or both. I also collect books by Baskerville, Bodoni and other eighteenth-century printers. Also nineteenth-century travel books."

The library room itself was built about 200 years ago by General John Campbell, who then owned the house. Sir Fitzroy admits that there are several other rooms in the house full of books. "I have had a lot of bookshelves built in the past and am having more built at the moment." Can he find what he wants here? Like all committed library users, the question is absurd. "I find my books by instinct." ∽

above

THE COMPLETE WORKS OF ENGLISH, AMERICAN, AND IRISH WRITERS
CREATE THE MELLOW BANDS OF COLOR THAT FRAME THE ROSENBLATT
FAMILY DINING ROOM/LIBRARY. ROGER HOLDS HECTOR, WHO AS A
PUPPY WAS FOND OF "DIGESTING" AN OCCASIONAL BOOK, MOST
NOTABLY A PRIZED 1911 EDITION OF THE ENCYCLOPAEDIA BRITANNICA,
SEEN AT RIGHT.

Roger Rosenblatt

Books are what we are. We carry them as we do our names. They give our lives order," says award-winning writer, journalist, editor, television essayist, and once-in-a-while playwright Roger Rosenblatt.

"Books are a storehouse of memories quite apart from their content. The passion begins in our youth and we die clutching the things," he writes and narrates in his monologue *Bibliomania*. "Leigh Hunt," he tells us, "wanted to be caught dead holding a book. He was. Plato was reputedly found dead with a book under his pillow; Petrarch with his elbow resting on an open page.

"Much of one's history is bound up with one's library and the books we read at different stages of our lives," Roger Rosenblatt says as he leads you through the book rooms of his grand old Belnord apartment on the Upper West Side of Manhattan. In lieu of a traditional library, he and his wife, Ginny, made room for books in virtually every room of the house. Roger's collections track his interests and his career, and read like the time line of his book-enthralled life.

Shelves display books given as childhood gifts, literature and criticism from his graduate years at Harvard, research books he started to collect when he was a student at New York University, the hundreds of books he reviews for the Pulitzer Prize Committee, a collection of Irish literature he assembled during his Fulbright year in Ireland, and the books he has written, notably *Children of War*, published in 1983 and translated into seven languages.

The room Roger calls his "reading retreat" contains prized books of old and modern poetry, fiction, and art. It's the place he heads for when he wants to unwind and break away from writing projects. "I use books as my source of knowledge, so when I read a book solely out of personal desire, I feel like a child again. It's rejuvenating." Frequently he chooses poetry. "It's not distracting and can be enjoyed for itself," he remarks as he retrieves Samuel Johnson's *Vanity of Human Wishes*.

"We like surrounding ourselves with books. They make better wall decorations than paintings," Roger volunteers, adding, "I especially like sets." He buys sets of books even when he's not particularly interested in all of a writer's works, believing that "if someone wrote something great the chances are he wrote other good things nobody paid attention to." He recalls a collection of Galsworthy he bought for twenty dollars and another by George Moore that he found in a furniture auction house. The Moore set is anchored in his extensive collection of Irish literature, joining Synge, Behan, Yeats, and Colum. The Galsworthy set enriched another section containing the complete works of Byron, Kipling, Boswell, Eliot, and Conrad, Roger's favorite novelist.

Although Roger says he does not separate the books he reads for pleasure from the ones he refers to as "utilitarian," he reserved the passageway leading to his workroom for books on film, television, radio, comedy, and show business. Dictionaries on early English, mythology, science, politics, and an array of McGraw-Hill reference books are positioned within arm's reach of his typewriter.

The phrase "you can read him like a book" comes to mind as you survey shelves filled with the collected works of Abraham Lincoln, the Modern Library Series old and new, and a passageway framed with pen-and-ink drawings of celebrated writers. Antique book-related accessories abound in every room. A book tray holds six volumes of Charles Lamb, a blacksmith's tool trolley was adopted for Chaucer's *Poetical Works*. A table holds a faux book of postcard portraits of English writers.

Bibliophilia ran in the Rosenblatt family. "My parents had floor-to-ceiling bookshelves. I climbed them like a ladder, staring at the titles I could not yet read, flinging the books down to the floor where I could look at them. I didn't understand most of what was written, but I just liked the books as objects. They were boxes of secrets," Roger reminisces. "Most influential were three women who lived above my family's apartment in Gramercy Park. They lived in a kind of antique splendor among their books. I would climb up the back stairs in through the kitchen. Their apartment was filled with low shelves that went around an L-shaped room. Each would read to me from her favorite children's books: *Wind in the Willows, Tom Sawyer, Huckleberry Finn,*

and *Dr. Dolittle*. In the forties people read books and they read to their children. There was no television; it wasn't regarded by either party as anything special. That was my good luck.

"These generous women read to me, my parents read to me, and so of course my wife and I read to our children. Ours was a family library. We never separated the children's books from our books. No book was ever 'off limits.' It wasn't necessary. I never collected many rare books because in a way I don't believe in them. I don't find a first edition any different from a thirtieth unless somebody's changed it."

Roger expresses dismay when he notices a missing volume. "I probably loaned it to somebody," he says with a shrug. "It makes me sore. Charles Lamb was right when he called book borrowers 'mutilators of collections, spoilers of the symmetry of shelves, and creators of odd volumes.' The interesting thing about the feeling of loss when a book is borrowed is that the book's quality rarely matters. So mysterious is the power of books in our lives that every loss is a serious loss, every hole in the shelf a crater. Our books are ourselves, our characters, our insulation against those very people who would take away our books. Someone should invent markers for bookcases to note 'missing persons.'"

Roger also reveals strong feelings about everything from people who write marginal notes in a book to what makes a great bookstore. "I write notes in my books all the time, believing that it adds value to them. I learned this at Harvard, where library books record the comments of students going back a hundred years. I even found Henry James's name in one of them." As to the best library, Roger says the test should be, Could you fall in love there? ✑

Bibliomania

The custom of borrowing books confutes nature. In every other such situation, the borrower becomes a slave to the lender, the social weight of the debt so altering the balance of a relationship that a temporary acquisition turns into a permanent loss. This is certainly true with money. Yet it is not at all true with books. For some reason a book borrower feels that a book, once taken, is his own. This removes both memory and guilt from the transaction. Making matters worse, the lender believes it, too. To keep up appearances, he may solemnly extract an oath that the book be brought back as soon as possible; the borrower answering with matching solemnity that the Lord might seize his eyes were he to do otherwise. But it is all play. Once gone, the book is gone forever. The lender, fearing rudeness, never asks for it again. The borrower never stoops to raise the subject.

Can book borrowers be thwarted? There are attempts. Some hopeful people glue stickers that read EX LIBRIS to the inside covers (clever drawings of animals wearing glasses, adorable yet pointless, and the name of the owner: "EX LIBRIS Rosenblattimus")—as if the presence of Latin and the imprint of a name were so formidable as to reverse a motor reflex. It never works. One might try slipping false jackets on one's books—a cover for *Cry the Beloved Country* disguising a book actually entitled *Utility Rates in Ottawa: A Woman's View.*

There's no spectacle that is as terrifying as the sight of a guest in your house whom you catch staring at your books. It is not the judgmental possibility that is frightening. The fact that one's sense of discrimination is exposed by his books. Indeed, most people would much prefer to see the guest first scan, then peer and turn away in boredom or disapproval. Alas, too often the eyes, dark with calculation, shift from title to title as from floozie to floozie in an overheated dance hall. Nor is that the worst. It is when those eyes stop moving that the heart, too, stops.

The guest's body twitches; his hand floats up to where his eyes have led it. There is nothing to be done. You freeze. He smiles. You hear the question even as it forms: "Would you mind if I borrowed this book?"

Mind? Why should I mind? The fact that I came upon that book in a Paris bookstall in April 1969—the 13th, I believe it was, the afternoon, it was drizzling—that I found it after searching all Europe and North America for a copy; that it is dog-eared at passages that mean more to my life than my heartbeat; that the mere touch of its pages recalls to me in a Proustian shower my first love, my best dreams. Should I mind that you seek to take all that away? That I will undoubtedly never get it back? Then even if you actually return it to me one day, I will be wizened, you cavalier, and the book spoiled utterly by your mishandling? *Mind?*

"Not at all. Hope you enjoy it."

"Thanks. I'll bring it back next week."

"No rush. Take your time." [Liar.]

This excerpt is from Bibliomania, *a one-man show written and performed by Roger Rosenblatt and staged at New York's American Place Theatre in 1994.*

The Enemies of Books

THESE FINE ILLUSTRATIONS FOR A
PAMPHLET, "CARE FOR BOOKS,"
ORIGINALLY COMMISSIONED BY
PARSONS SCHOOL OF DESIGN, ARE
BY DAN CHATMAN.

In 1880 William Blades wrote his comprehensive *The Enemies of Books*. This classic, though filled with stern admonitions, is as relevant today as it was a century ago. Blades's work speaks to those who are building or restoring a library, starting a special collection, or those simply interested in preserving the books they read in their youth for their children and grandchildren. Just as people often think to create a protected environment for paintings or photographs, so should they for their books.

1   **Fire**

"There are many of the forces of Nature which tend to injure books; but among them all not one has been half as destructive as fire." — W.B.

Blades calculates that not only is fire the most destructive of all enemies of books, but that only one-thousandth of the books that once existed still exist, thanks to what he calls the "fire-king."

Good housekeeping, according to the National Fire Protection Association, is the number one way to prevent a fire. As in a forest deprived of rain, overly dry conditions are conducive to fire. Climate control through central air-conditioning can guard against the drying and dust-promoting power of heat. Some collectors use fireproof wastepaper baskets or containers and choose nonflammable and/or fire retardant material for library curtains and upholstery.

Smoking is as bad for books as it is for people. Not only does it increase the risk of fire because of a dropped ash or fallen match, but smoke can work its way into the pages of books and leave a smell behind. If you smoke, or have guests who do, be especially alert when you're in the library.

After studying the effects of a serious fire that caused considerable damage from heat, Don Etherington, former conservator at the Harry Ransom Humanities Research Center, found that books that had been oiled resisted heat better than those that had not been treated. The drier the book, the greater the damage. Leather bindings and labels, including those in glass-fronted cases, were frizzed or looked bubbled, particularly those stored on upper shelves where heat was most intense. A rapid decrease in humidity may be the reason for this. Leather bindings should be put on lower shelves even in glass-fronted cases where they are, in general, better protected. Polyester dust jackets are also a good book saver.

If fire or smoke does damage your books, there are materials that can help you repair them. Jane Greenfield, author of *The Care of Fine Books*, finds that Pink Pearl erasers work better than any other material for removing scorch marks. Damp sponges work best on smooth cloth, but do not work well on paper. Extra-fine steel wool will take soot off leather bindings and leave them intact. However, she says, "Beware of chemical sponges, which leave residual film. To get rid of any lingering smell after a fire, thoroughly air books out on a clear, slightly breezy day. Stand books, fanned out, on a table in the shade, but do not leave them overnight. Fire damage

restoration firms can also provide equipment to dissipate residual odor." To find such a firm in your area, check the Yellow Pages under "Fire and Water Damage Restoration."

2   **Water**

"Next to Fire we must rank Water in its two forms, liquid and vapour, as the greatest destroyer of books." — W.B.

Aside from flooding through natural disaster or otherwise, water vapor or general dampness can lead to mold and disfigured books. As Blades describes it, "Outside it fosters the growth of a white mould or fungus which vegetates upon the edges of the leaves, upon the sides and in the joints of the binding . . ."

Doris Hamburg, in *Caring for Your Collections*, notes the warning signs of dampness and methods of treatment. A musty smell and the appearance of fuzzy spores are the tip-offs. If mold develops, as it is prone to do in seaside houses or in basements, remove the affected books and place them in a dry area. Then, on a sunny day, take the books outside and lightly brush the mold with a soft camel-hair brush to remove the spores. Dabbing, but not rubbing, with a kneaded eraser will show whether the material is too delicate to be brushed. If so, or if in doubt, bring the books to a professional conservator.

Mold develops because of poor air circulation and too much humidity. So if you're keeping books in glass-fronted bookcases, make sure that you open them periodically to provide essential ventilation. Mold grows at 70° F. and 65 percent relative humidity in stagnant air. It can be prevented or controlled by maintaining a library temperature below 70° F. and by allowing relative humidity to climb no higher than 60 percent, preferably keeping it closer to

50 percent. Air conditioners and fans can be used for climate control. Dehumidifiers help through the warmer seasons. Humidifiers should be used in winter when a well-heated library also means too little humidity, which can dry out books and increase the risk of fire.

If you live in a house that tends to flood, keep your bookshelves at least twelve inches from the floor. Collector Timothy Mawson recalls the morning he came into his New York shop after such in-house flooding. "A water pipe broke in the men's room above and totally flooded everything. We used wax paper between the pages of the books so they would not stick together and worked at it for nearly forty-eight hours, saving an enormous number of books."

If your books get wet, those that are not absolutely saturated can be dried by fan. Stand the books on several layers of paper towels or unprinted newspaper (available at art supply stores) and let one or two fans blow on them. If possible, use a piece of Styrofoam under the opened book for support. Books can also be dried by placing paper towels or unprinted newspaper within the book, one every fifty pages or so. (Newspaper is a good absorber, but because of its acidic content it should not be left inside a book for too long.) The towels and/or newspaper should be changed often—a time-consuming operation. When books are almost dry (slightly cool to the cheek), close them and finish the drying under light weights. Softcover books can be dried this way or hung on a clothesline. (If your collection is seriously damaged by water, remind your insurance company that the longer wet books sit and mold forms, the higher the cost of restoration; this may hasten an appraisal.)

For books with coated paper, such as most illustrated books, freeze or vacuum drying is recommended. (This paper tends to stick together when wet and then dried by the usual methods.) Wrap such books in freezer paper and pack them tightly in plastic milk crates. While taking books to a rapid-freezing facility is best, a home freezer can be used. After the books are frozen, they should be kept at -15 to 20° F. until a vacuum-drying facility can take them to be dried. (In vacuum drying, water goes straight from ice to vapor.)

Very few facilities offer these techniques of freezing and vacuum drying. For addresses of those in your area, contact Wei T'O Associates, P.O. Drawer 40, 21750 Main Street, Unit 27, Matteson, IL 60443. (312) 747-6660. Also check the Yellow Pages under "Fire and Water Damage Restoration." For other conservation information, see the Resource Directory.

3   **Gas and Heat**

"Treat books as you should your own children, who are sure to sicken if confined in an atmosphere which is impure, too hot, too cold, too damp or too dry." — W.B.

Blades, writing about the twin dangers of gas and heat, had witnessed the damaging effect his gas lamps had on books stored on upper shelves. The sulphur in the gas fumes had turned them into the consistency "of scotch snuff." Today, air-conditioning and protective cases are the best guards against chemical threats.

Though chemicals such as sulphur dioxide and other air pollutants are a potent danger to books, heat alone can damage books by drying out and destroying their bindings. Heat, Jane Greenfield says, increases the deconstructive power of acid that may be lurking within a book's paper or ink, and causes a lowering of relative humidity.

Designer Jack Lenor Larsen recalls visiting an elegant library years ago and being told that four maids would apply Vaseline to all the leather bindings twice a year to prevent them from drying out. For those without four maids or a lot of free time, the best preventative to heat damage is to maintain a library temperature of between 60° and 70° F., preferably at the lower end of the scale, and to keep books away from radiators and other heat sources.

4   **Light**

"The electric light has been in use in the Reading Room of the British Museum, and is a great boon to the readers. However, you must choose particular positions if you want to work happily. There is a great objection too in the humming fizz which accompanies it . . . and there is still greater objection when small pieces of hot chalk fall on your head." — W.B.

Though Blades foresaw the downside of electric lighting for the reader, he did not foresee its particular dangers to the books themselves. "Light," Doris Hamburg writes, "causes changes in the paper structure itself as well as leading to bleaching, fading, darkening, and/or embrittlement." The ultraviolet rays in fluorescent lights can be damaging, explains Elaine Haas, president of TALAS, a professional resource center for libraries. If you have very valuable books, she suggests you slip special ultraviolet absorbent material over the fluorescent tubes.

But in addition to artificial light sources, sunlight can be equally or more damaging. Even indirect sunlight can lead to fading. An unpopular but simple way to protect your collection is to draw the blinds in your library. Food book collector Richmond Ellis uses window shades on the bookshelves themselves.

5   **Dust and Neglect**

"Dust upon Books to any extent points to Neglect, and neglect means more or less slow Decay." — W.B.

For those who hate to dust, there are storage options to avoid the problem. Jack Lenor Larsen adopted Japanese design practices and found that "if fabrics are hung up from the ceiling to cover the books I don't have to look at a lot of stuff all the time. It

also reduces dust and therefore cleaning and break-age." Window shades can also protect books from dust and other pollutants. Make sure any material you use is acid-free. Protective book boxes can preserve rare books from dust or pollution.

There is no formula for how often a library must be dusted; it depends on the environment. Anthony Trollope dusted his library twice a year. Frequent vacuuming and/or sweeping will reduce dust build-up. Most dust collects at the top edges of books. A feather duster is the classic implement for removing dust, but a vacuum cleaner is better. A portable mini-vac, or Dustbuster, though less powerful, may be easier to use in the small spaces between books. Barbara Kirschenblatt-Gimblett uses something in between—a Service Vacuum Cleaner she ordered through Contact East, Inc., North Andover, Massachusetts. Designed for cleaning delicate office equipment like computers, disk drives, and printers, this vacuum is portable and relatively light, weighing a total of nine pounds.

Regardless of the method you choose, Jane Greenfield recommends you begin by cleaning the top edge of the book. Dust and vacuum away from

the spine and hold the book tightly so the dust does not work its way down into the pages. You can use saddle soap on leather bindings to remove dust, dirt, and grime, but not on gold tooling or turn-ins (leather-bound books whose binding extends within the inside edges of the covers and spine). Any moisture can cause blackening and cracking of deteriorating leather, so only clean them if you have to. If you decide to clean your leather bindings, form a lather with the saddle soap and rub the lather into the leather. Wipe off the excess with a clean, damp sponge, drying the binding with a lint-free cloth. Let the book dry completely before putting it back. For cloth bindings, you can use Bookleen Gel, available from library resources (see Resource Directory). For rare paper bindings, expert help may be required, such as described in Anne F. Clapp's book, *Curatorial Care of Works of Art on Paper: Basic Procedures for Paper Preservation.*

6   **Ignorance**

> *"Ten years ago, when turning out an old closet in the Mazarine Library, of which I am librarian, I discovered at the bottom, under a lot of old rags and rubbish, a large volume. It had no cover nor title-page, and had been used to light the fires of librarians."* — W.B.

Even the best-educated bibliophiles, like author and journalist Roger Rosenblatt, are torn between their respect for books and their desire to enjoy them to their fullest, for instance, by engaging with the text through scrawled commentary. "It's shameful to admit: I deface books all the time," he says, referring to his penciled scribbles. "And I enjoy seeing the scribbling of others. There is a communicative and emotional value in a record of another human being's thoughts and feelings left for future readers to happen upon. Of course, though this harms a book, if the scribbler happens to have been Henry James or James Joyce the book becomes much more valuable."

Books can also be damaged by people's well-meaning efforts to repair them, particularly by using nonrestoration-quality material, such as transparent or duct tape to repair torn pages or bindings. Bookbinders have to use Unseal Adhesive Releasing Solvent to remove such tape from books. If you do not wish to take a damaged book to a professional restorer, binders Wilton Wiggins and Douglas Lee advise you to wrap the book in acid-free paper and tie it up with library tape, a flat cotton string that can be used to hold the book together if the spine or binding is loose. There are also special tapes available in a first-aid kit from Talas in New York (see Resource Directory) and other resources.

The Bookworm (and Other Vermin)

"There is a sort of busy worm
That will the fairest books deform,
By gnawing holes throughout them.
Alike, through every leaf they go,
Yet of its merit nought they know,
Nor care they aught about them.

Their tasteless tooth will tear and taint
The Poet, Patriot, Sage or Saint,
Nor sparing wit nor learning.
Now, if you'd know the reason why,
The best of reasons I'll supply:
'Tis bread to the poor vermin."

J. Doraston (quoted by William Blades)

Worms, beetles, and creepy-crawlies of all kinds can chomp through your precious volumes and turn them into fodder—and birthing places for larvae. "If," Jane Greenfield says, "you have termites in your bookshelves, or if you are stacking books from suspect areas, like barns, cellars, and attics, you should freeze the collection before placing it in your library." She reports that a simple at-home method was developed by Yale University biology professor Charles Remington: Make sure the books are completely dry, thereby preventing the formation of ice crystals. Seal books or wrap them well in plastic bags, preferably made of polyethylene, and freeze them at 6° F. in a domestic freezer. (At Yale, books are frozen at -20° F. for seventy-two hours.) This will kill all beetles and insects at all stages of development. For more information, see the Resource Directory. ∾

Library Ladders

opposite

LADDER MERCHANTS GREGG AND
WARREN MONSEES SIT FOR A
PORTRAIT IN FRONT OF PUTNAM
ROLLING LADDER COMPANY, THE
FAMILY-OWNED BUSINESS THAT HAS
BECOME A SOHO LANDMARK.

above

THE STATUS LIBRARY ACCESSORY,
THE ELEPHANT (POLE) LADDER IS
AVAILABLE THROUGH THE EXIMIOUS
OF LONDON CATALOG (SEE
RESOURCE DIRECTORY).

When books take over your life and start climbing the walls, it's time for a library ladder. Books you love, plan to reread, or need for reference should never be out of reach. Standing on chairs, beds, or kitchen stools to retrieve books banished to the top shelves is no substitute for a sturdy, stable library ladder. Best of all, ladders are accommodating. They come in all sizes, shapes, styles, periods (modern and antique) and in a variety of woods, finishes, and models. Some ladders are designed, like furniture, to grace a reading room. None is more intriguing than the elephant (pole) ladder used to mount pachyderms in India and later adopted by the British to scale the book-clad walls of their Georgian homes. Closed, it becomes a beautifully crafted column of wood that announces: "A bibliophile lives here." Other ladders, more practical for contemporary small-space living, have been designed to double as chairs and side tables. Some have been constructed to fold up for stowing away.

One of the best places to view and shop for ladders for "every climbing need" is the Putnam Rolling Ladder Company. Named for its founder Samuel Putnam, this turn-of-the-century storehouse for ladders has been at the same location at 32 Howard Street in Lower Manhattan for over forty years. Ladders of infinite variety fill a five-story cast-iron

AN ANTIQUE LADDER CHAIR IN SEYMOUR DURST'S "OLD YORK LIBRARY," POSITIONED TO REACH HIS WELL-STACKED SHELVES.

building that is a magnet for decorators, merchants, photographers, utility companies, architects, and homeowners from all over the country and abroad.

The top floor is devoted to vintage ladders that co-owners Warren and Gregg Monsees (father and son) assemble and restore to sell to interior designers for period rooms or rent to theater and film companies staging historical productions.

Their trademark product, the rolling ladder, occupies still another floor. It's the ladder you remember seeing in department stores or neighborhood libraries when you were a child. Today, it's the ubiquitous ladder we're once again seeing in bookstores that opt for a retro look, in chain stores that need to maximize vertical space, and, for the same reason, in the libraries of residential lofts and high-ceiling homes.

The rolling ladder the Monsees tag "Putnam #1" dates back to 1905, when the store first opened. It remains one of their most popular ladders, drawing buyers from as far away as Japan and Australia. Still available in its original clear red oak, it also comes in a variety of different woods, including cherry, walnut, maple, ash, or Honduras mahogany, and can be finished with a patina of age. Rolling ladders can be ordered to reach any height, with a variety of caster and track styles to satisfy library decor and dimensions. To conserve space, Putnam #1 has a top slide feature that permits it to be pushed out for climbing and pushed back against the shelves when not in use.

Gregg Monsees explains that a 9-foot, 16-inch-wide rolling ladder made of oak with an oak finish, brass-plated features, and a 10-foot track would cost

about $575. Extras, such as old-fashioned metal casters, special track finishes, safety brakes, and handrails are available for an additional charge.

The storefront floor of Putnam Rolling Ladder showcases a diversity of ladder and library products from book stools to Putnam #70. This ladder, which folds in on itself for convenient storage, dates back to Thomas Jefferson's time, and sketches of it can be found in his archives. Lightweight but sturdy platform ladders come with handrails and are a contemporary version of the custom-made pulpit ladder Joseph Mindel has in his 5,000-volume Edwardian library. "Decorator stools" range from practical stepstools that provide extra reach to handle-back models that convert into pull-up library chairs for comfortable book browsing. They are today's version of the antique ladder chair in Seymour Durst's "Old York Library."

There's a ladder for every taste and pocketbook from Cramer's "Kik-Step," a utility metal stepstool available in office supply stores like Staples, to a turn-of-the-century rolling ladder, found in antique stores or auction houses. See Resource Directory for details. ℰℬ

PRIVATE PLEASURES

Reading Retreats

AN SHOULD TREASURE BOOKS BECAUSE—THEY HAVE GUIDED HIM TO TRUTH; THEY HAVE FILLED HIS MIND WITH NOBLE AND GRACEFUL IMAGES; THEY STOOD BY HIM IN ALL VICISSITUDES, COMFORTERS IN SORROW, NURSES IN SICKNESS, COMPANIONS IN SOLITUDE. &

—THOMAS MACAULAY

KEITH RICHARDS

PETER CANNELL

WALTER AND JANE TURKEN

KITTY D'ALESSIO

FLORA AND SYDNEY BIDDLE

MICHAEL AND AILEEN CASEY

"LIBRI," TROMPE L'OEIL MULTICOLORED FABRIC DESIGNED BY PIERO FORNASETTI—BLUMENTHAL, INC.

Keith Richards

"After a life on the road, reading anchors me."

How could a Rolling Stone own a library? When does a Rolling Stone buy books? He is on the road much of the year, he lives in several places at once, he is possessed by his guitar and the sounds he plucks from it. Yet there is nothing more satisfying to Keith Richards than to be lying on his sofa, buried in a book, in his very own library.

The house he owns in rural Connecticut is huge, bright, with high ceilings and bleached floors. In such a house one might imagine a classically proportioned library with skylights and light wood paneling. Keith Richards had something else in mind. "I didn't want a large room. I wanted a small room with a high ceiling that would be all *mine*." So in this light-filled house he found for himself a corner in which he designed a rich, dark space proportioned to his taste.

The octagonal shape was carefully thought out, its windows angled to receive the afternoon western sun. (Like most performers, he is rarely up and about in the mornings.) He oversaw every aspect of the library: its size, shelving, the kind of wood, the furnishings. He loves this place.

"When you are growing up, there are two institutional places that affect you most powerfully—the church, which belongs to God, and the public library, which belongs to you. The public library is a great equalizer. As a child, you get to feel all these books are yours." Keith, an only child, was encouraged by his parents to read, and now passes that encouragement on to his children. "I was living in Switzerland and used to read to my son. But there were not many English books so I had to buy French ones. I taught myself the language by making it up from looking at the pictures. My son would say, 'Are you sure that's what happened, Dad?' Now my children always want me to make up the stories. For instance, we have a book about cats and the kids want me to say what the cats are saying in the pictures."

Mr. Richards's dependence on books became acute once he became part of the Rolling Stones band. "On planes it's awful not to have something to read. So much of being on tour is boredom. Reading is the antidote of boredom," according to Mr. Richards. His reading is eclectic: "I can read anything except a book

One of his major interests is history, and in particular the Nazi period. He also has a large number of books on military strategy. Why this interest? "If I weren't interested, I'd be dead by now," he says with a grin. "I work in front of hundreds of thousands of people, all screaming and raving. Dictators have the same effect. I'm interested in how people can fall for dictators, and in the origins of the mass psychosis they provoke. That's what I do for a living, after all. Time to go to the office—go out in front of hordes of howling people! I'm fascinated by the transformation of a person going on stage. You become part of the mass hysteria. You forget yourself in the moment. Is that what Hitler experienced?"

When he was a child, there was no library at home. He usually had to read in a corner of a room or in an attic. "I'm still not used to having this great retreat," he says with pleasure. "I see now why eighteenth-century English gentlemen had them. It's my sanctuary." He means it. No one, not even the children, can just walk in on Dad when he's in his library. There is a sign on the door he lifted from the Savoy Hotel in London that says DO NOT DISTURB. "That didn't work," Richards says ruefully. "I had to change it to DO NOT ENTER."

Keith Richards has never been longer than two months in one place for over twenty-five years. "Reading keeps me in one spot," he says. "After a life on the road, reading anchors me." As he enters into the intimate, moody atmosphere of his private cave for reading, for a few moments the Rolling Stone gathers moss. ❧

with pages missing." His library contains most of the major nineteenth- and twentieth-century novelists, plus espionage, history, art books. "Like most rock-and-roll artists I did my time at art school." Not surprisingly, considering his profession, Keith Richards's library contains records as well as books. He has books on guitars and other musical instruments, but not many. "Music is to listen to," he says.

A DETECTIVE WOULD FIND LITTLE DIFFICULTY IN GUESSING AT THE
PERSONALITY OF THE OWNER OF THIS DESK.

IN HIS OCTAGONAL LIBRARY WITH MAHOGANY TRIM AND CLASSICAL
MOTIFS CARVED BY EASTERN EUROPEAN CARPENTERS, A FIREPLACE,
AND RICH, DARK COBALT AND BURGUNDY HANGINGS, KEITH
RICHARDS KEEPS BOREDOM (AND CHILDREN) AT BAY.

Peter Cannell

"YOUR BOOKS ARE YOUR PERSONAL HISTORY.

YOU ARE WHAT YOU READ."

The minute Peter Cannell gets into his car at 5:30 A.M. for his daily commute to New York City from Long Island, he turns on his car tape player—and listens to a book. "I listen to nothing but books," he says. "Right now I am deep into *Rumpole for the Defence*." The reason for Rumpole is that the novel is read by Patrick Tull, a reader to whom Mr. Cannell has become devoted. "Some people in horse racing play the jockey," he explains. "I play the reader." So far, he has listened to Patrick Tull read *Hard Times* and *Pickwick Papers,* and expects to hear more.

Peter Cannell's own reading is done at home in the country, in the library/studio designed in the neoclassical tradition of curved libraries by the architectural firm of Cicognani Kalla. The most dramatic twentieth-century example of the circular library is the public library in Stockholm, which was the inspiration for this one.

"It is very satisfying to be able to see all the books at once," says Pietro Cicognani. "A curved library achieves this." His firm has made something of a specialty out of library design; the library at the

newly opened Heinz Architectural Center in Pittsburgh is a spectacular example.

The Cannells started building their house approximately five years ago, and the architects were given free rein as to the layout. The original plan was to have the library walls part of a double-storied living room, but Mr. Cannell, who does a lot of his work as an investment adviser at home, required a work space as well. Thus the insertion of the platform floor above the living room. But the architects wanted something more interesting than the simple two-level solution. They built a curved passageway of books on one level (allowing enough shelf space for additional volumes) and then created a three-foot step section that goes down into the study area. This separation of space allows the visitor to stroll along the passage, "grazing" the books, without disturbing the worker at his desk. At the far end of this literary promenade, there is a little doorway leading out on to an Italianate balcony and a view of the pastoral landscape.

"It was clear this library should not be closed off from such a wonderful view of the outdoors," says architect Cicognani. With the curved wall of

opposite

THE SPECIALLY DESIGNED LIBRARY LIGHTING BY CICOGNANI KALLA IS MADE OF STEEL, THE ANTIQUE PATINA BLENDING WELL WITH THE COLORED BOOK JACKETS THE LIGHTS ILLUMINATE.

above

THE CURVED LIBRARY OFFERS VIEWS LIKE A REVOLVING

RESTAURANT, AS WELL AS CREATES SPACE IN THE CENTER

UP A SMALL STAIRCASE.

below left

OFF THE LIBRARY IS A LITTLE ALCOVE FOR PRIVACY WHILE READING

OR BROWSING.

below right

AT ONE END OF THE LIBRARY, A DOOR OPENS ONTO A BALCONY AND

A PRETTY VIEW OF THE GARDEN OUTSIDE.

books at one's back, one looks out of the huge windows opposite onto the gardens and lawns of the house almost as though viewing a movie. Light pours into the main well of the study area from these windows. The books also have their own custom-made lights integrated into the shelving, giving a uniform wash of light on the surface of the books. At night, when the windows are dark, the books glow with a hospitable warmth.

Most of the Cannell family's books are stored here, fiction on the left, nonfiction on the right, all alphabetized. Sections on advertising and financial subjects indicate Peter Cannell's particular interests. "Your books are your personal history," he says. "You are what you read."

The clearest evidence of this is the occasional appearance on these shelves of more than one copy of the same book. That is because Peter Cannell, although not a rare book collector ("like stocks, you don't buy them if you don't know anything about them"), tends to acquire several copies of his favorite books. He has three or four copies, for instance, of *The Lawrenceville Stories* by Owen Johnson, *By Love Possessed* by James Gould Cozzens, and *Luce and His Empire,* the biography of Henry Luce by W. A. Swanberg. "These are inspirational books, at least to me, and after convivial evenings, I tend to give my extra copies away." What an agreeable solution to the problem of lending one's treasured books that never get returned. You just give them away instead! ⁌

IN THIS FORMER GRISTMILL, THE ORIGINAL CHESTNUT BEAMS,

STENCILED CEILING BY KARL SMITH, AND NINETEENTH-CENTURY

ENGLISH LIBRARY TABLE PROVIDE A WONDERFUL SETTING FOR THE

TURKENS' LIBRARY.

Walter and Jane Turken

"I WAS SO HAPPY TO SEE A READY-MADE PLACE FOR ALL MY BOOKS."

Gristmills tend to have threshing floors and millraces. But when Jane Turken first saw the main living room of this converted mill, all she saw was the bookshelves. "My favorite thing is to read," she says. "I was so happy to see a ready-made place for all my books."

It was not quite as simple as that, of course. The gristmill, originating from 1681 and converted by previous owners, was not in good working order when Jane and her husband, real-estate developer Walter Turken, bought the place. Two years of renovation were embarked on with the help of interior designer Juan Montoya, who raised ceilings, installed insulation and new heating systems, firmed up and refinished floors, and found furniture and furnishings that would reflect the Mission-style brick and wood theme of the old mill building.

In the living room the original roof and floor beams were kept, with stenciling added to the ceiling panels. Kilim rugs and upholstery gave warmth to the former barn. As for the library wall, its old beams were treasures beyond price. The only change the Turkens made was to thicken each shelf, so as to give better support to the books and also enhance the proportions.

Both the Turkens love to read, and they taught their children this love. "I think it's passed down through families." Jane Turken buys books, often on recommendation. "Friends say, 'Jane, you must read this.' I often buy just by reading the jacket copy."

Unlike some readers, Jane Turken doesn't read in bed. "When I go to bed I'm usually so tired I fall right asleep. And with the sound of the waterfall outside, it's even easier." She reads during the day, on the sofa, or outside, using one of her dogs as a headrest. "Old English love stories, historical romances that have a mixture of fiction and nonfiction; give me one of those and I melt." ✂

above

JANE TURKEN FINDS A COMFORTABLE HEADREST FOR READING BY THE WATERFALL.

Kitty D'Alessio

"THERE ARE SOME BOOKS I'D NEVER GIVE AWAY.

I'M ALWAYS RUNNING OUT OF SHELF SPACE."

A Portault-dressed bed, piled high with heirloom linen "reading pillows" and bracketed by tables toppling with books, book tapes, magazines, and family pictures faces a commanding fireplace-centered book wall in Kitty D'Alessio's bedroom/library.

"A home for my books was the first thing that came to mind when I saw the floor-through space created when the Warburg family converted their double brownstone into a few apartments. The library wall was here when I moved in," Kitty recalls. "All I had to do was add an ebony stain to the walnut shelves. I wanted a black frame to set off and calm the colorful book jackets and book bindings I would see from my bed."

Kitty's self-described "literary lair" also serves as a private sitting room and study with across-the-room access to the books she selects to have close by when she's working at home or in bed, her preferred place for reading.

Tastemaker, arbiter of style, and businesswoman (D'Alessio broke through Chanel's glass ceiling and became its president in 1979), Kitty is a relentless acquirer of books that mirror her interests and activities: art, business, fashion, architecture, decor, biography, history, theater, and film. She frequently calls on her favorite book finders, Shaun Gunison and Jane Stubbs, to track down out-of-print titles or books published abroad.

"My system for collecting and cataloging my books is personal. It works for me," Kitty says. "I organize my books by field of interest and writers of importance to me. There are some books I'd never give away and they're the ones I arrange in my library/bedroom, books like the Durants' *Age of Reason* and Will Durant's series *The Story of Civilization.*

opposite

D'ALESSIO BUILT A CORRIDOR OF BOOKS TO HOUSE HER COLLECTION, EASILY ACCESSIBLE AS SHE MOVES FROM BEDROOM TO LIVING ROOM.

above

A FIREPLACE-CENTERED EBONY BOOK WALL IS THE VISUAL

CENTERPIECE OF A BEDROOM DESIGNED FOR THE RECLUSIVE

PLEASURES OF READING, WRITING, AND REFLECTION.

below

A BOOK COLLECTOR'S SECRETAIRE OF VINTAGE PROVENANCE
CONTAINS EXQUISITELY BOUND BOOKS, HANDCRAFTED
STATIONERY, AND ANTIQUE WRITING IMPLEMENTS.

A book I read and reread is Curtis Bill Pepper's recollections of Pope John XIII, *An Artist and the Pope.*

"I'm always running out of shelf space, despite the fact that I adopted two feet of the interior stairwell to create a corridor book wall inside my apartment. Now this walkway that joins my bedroom/library and living room is lined floor-to-ceiling with books I'm constantly buying or people are giving me to update my business research library. They include books on Indian and Japanese culture, gardening, health, and home that I've been touched by. Periodically, I'll select the books I no longer read and pass them on to friends, family, colleagues, or college libraries, among them the Fashion Institute of Technology. It gives me the space I need for the new books that keep my library and me current."

Kitty D'Alessio never questions the cost of a book if she wants it, and while she frequents independent booksellers like the Madison Avenue Bookshop, she also shops book discounters for titles of less lasting value to her. To afford all the books she wants to read, Kitty D'Alessio and several of her friends created their own book co-op. They take turns buying books they want to read and then pass them on to each other. "This," she explains, "makes even the most expensive book affordable and the more enjoyable because it expands the opportunity to discuss a shared reading interest." ↩

ARCHITECT MICHAEL GRAVES CREATED THE ILLUSION OF SPACE IN
THE BIDDLE LIBRARY/LIVING ROOM BY LINING WALLS WITH
RECESSED ALCOVES TO MAKE ROOM FOR BOOKS, ART, FAMILY, AND A
MULTITUDE OF ARTIST AND WRITER FRIENDS.

Flora and Sydney Biddle

"HOUSES DON'T REMAIN, BUT BOOKS DO."

I grew up in very horse country and read innumerable books about horses," Flora Biddle, chairman of the Whitney Museum of American Art, recalls. "I couldn't wait until the next birthday or Christmas so I could get another book. I can still picture those books today.

"I had my own library in my bedroom with a complete set of *The Wizard of Oz* that I loved," she once wrote in tribute to her mother, Flora Whitney Miller, the driving force in the expansion of the Whitney. "Both my mother and grandmother were avid readers and enjoyed reading aloud. Mother would read books to me when I was sick or at bedtime. Kipling's Jungle Books about Mowgli or *The White Seal* were favorites. She would tell me how 'Gammoo,' my grandmother, read them to her when she was a child. I, in turn, read to my mother years later in a cornstalk blind on a dove shoot in Aiken, South Carolina."

The custom of reading books to one another has been passed on from generation to generation. Children's books Flora reads to her grandchildren are scattered on tables and chairs in the living room/library of the Biddles' nineteenth-century carriage house in New York. They are as prominent as the limited edition series of *Artists and Writers* books Flora Biddle encouraged the Whitney to publish sev-

eral years ago and proudly positions for viewing on a large table that centers the room. Voracious readers, Flora and Sydney Biddle buy books independently, then share their discoveries by reading passages to each other, propped up in bed with the "comfort pillows" Flora had made for just this purpose. "The bedroom is our favorite reading haunt," Sydney reveals. "It's where we share book space. There are books on each of the bedside tables and books on the floor on both sides of the bed.

"Books have been a strong force in the lives of both our families," Sydney adds. "My grandmother was an eccentric woman. After her wedding she went to bed to finish reading a French novel. Now that's what I call a dedicated reader."

"I was made aware of my family's artistic tradition early on," Flora explains. "My grandmother, Gertrude Vanderbilt Whitney, began the museum in 1930 and it came to symbolize the creative and enduring aspects of our lives."

Flora has been associated with the museum since 1958 and is a passionate supporter of the collaboration of American artists and writers. To help raise money for the Whitney's book-publishing fund, she encouraged the museum to publish hand-printed, specially bound books that are sold to collectors and libraries. "It's really a wonderful conjunction of art

above

BOOKS CREATED BY ARTISTS AS GIFTS FOR FLORA AND *FLORA*, THE
BOOK SHE COMMISSIONED IN HOMAGE TO HER MOTHER, GRACE THE
BIEDERMEIER LIBRARY TABLE THAT ECHOES THE ROTUNDA CEILING
THAT GIVES LOFT TO THEIR FLOOR-THROUGH CARRIAGE HOUSE.

below

FLORA AND HER MOTHER, FLORA WHITNEY MILLER, SHARE THE
PLEASURE OF READING ON THE FRONT STEPS OF THEIR FAMILY
HOME IN AIKEN, SOUTH CAROLINA, IN 1933.

and literature, two of my loves, expressed through the medium of a book. I've always enjoyed the way books look, especially the old cloth-covered books that have been passed down to me or the modern ones with those wonderful book jackets that add to the art world we live in."

The Biddles live just a short walk away from the Whitney in a historic book-filled house that Flora's great-grandfather first occupied in the 1880s. When Michael Graves was designing the controversial expansion to Marcel Breuer's Whitney, the Biddles commissioned him to renovate their home as well.

"From the outset," Flora says, "we knew we wouldn't have as many shelves as we needed but we hoped Michael would create room for the books we kept without creating rows and rows of bookshelves. The first thing he asked us was, 'How many books do you and Sydney have?' We explained that we needed maximum space for our books and art, but also room enough to entertain for the museum."

Graves balanced the Biddles' needs by creating an illusion of space that accommodates books, art, and people. Recessed shelves were built into preexisting walls and others created with wood and plasterboard. The illusion is further reinforced by the "inlaid" treasury of hand-tooled volumes and the legacy of books Flora reserved for herself and her children when ancestral possessions were auctioned at Sotheby's. Artwork and sculpture from twentieth-century artists and pieces created by family members add intimacy.

"We've made three major moves over the last few years and have a great deal of experience on how to transport books in great quantities. We pack all

our books by subject, because that's the way we shelve them and it's much easier to unpack them that way. Over the years we've had to give away a lot of books; we gave boxes and boxes to hospitals and stored many more in our basement. We shipped others we knew we would miss to our second home in New Mexico. I couldn't wait to unpack them. There's something so wonderful about being able to look and touch the books you have, but you have to be selective about the ones you hold on to. I've held on to all my art books because I need them for my museum work."

Sydney counters, "I'm for giving away books that you haven't read in ten years. Then you don't have to move them. It's been said that houses don't remain but books do and I guess our lives prove it." (Flora and Sydney have moved from their Michael Graves–designed carriage house to a book-filled apartment in New York City.) ℘

Michael and Aileen Casey

"IT IS A TERRIBLE THING TO HAVE EDUCATED EYES

BUT A DEPLETED BANK ACCOUNT."

Romantic, mysterious, dilapidated, stylish—there is something wonderfully Irish about this library. The house in which it dwells, at one time housing up to 100 tenants, was built on the north side of Dublin in 1740 and was lived in for a while by two consecutive bishops before falling on hard times.

A young and enthusiastic couple, Michael and Aileen Casey, bought the house twenty years ago and were in the process of restoring it when this picture was taken. Restoring may seem too strong a word. The house was in such a shambles that it had no hot water and only one small toilet perched precariously on a half-landing. "When we came, the entire system had been blocked by a pair of cement-filled jeans," Aileen Casey reported, cheerfully reminding one of the kind of life this house had under its reign of squatters.

Scraping nineteen coats of paint off the walls, they discovered a delicious blue that dates back to the house's eighteenth century origins. Replacing mantelpieces, staircases and moldings with the help of the Irish Georgian Society was a major project for years. "I believe we are closer to the eighteenth-century feel of the rooms now than we will be when it is all painted and the details picked out," said the Caseys. Michael used to show visitors a chamber pot out of a cupboard built into the wall behind a shutter. "This is what they used after dinner, and they naturally threw the contents out of the window into the street below (still unpaved at that time), which was much more sensible than throwing it into one's own back garden."

With three children and much more imagination than cash, the Caseys lovingly transformed a structural disaster into living history. This library, with its walls steeped in poetry like Ireland itself, proudly acknowledges its infamous past and its hopeful future. ✧

opposite

IN A CORNER OF THE LIBRARY, AN EIGHTEENTH-CENTURY PORTRAIT

SHARES SPACE WITH MARBLE BUSTS AND STACKS OF LITERATURE.

Great Libraries

For many people, the first introduction to books came through a visit to the local public library. Not only artists, poets, and novelists, but everyday readers have been inspired by the world of discoveries within the perfect democracy of book stacks winding through the mysterious recesses of the public library. Many of the bibliophiles featured in these pages describe their first epiphanies of reading by being taken as children to the local library and picking out a book.

Sometimes these institutions are tiny one-room spaces with books squeezed together in a wasteland dominated by graffiti and the detritus of poverty. Others are soaring, timeless edifices, ornamented with gold and stained glass, such as the two cathedrals to books in the Strahov monastery in Prague, Czechoslovakia. Public libraries all serve the same humanitarian purpose, legislated by a benign government for the people's good—they offer a place where anyone, any time, may go and read, or take home, a book.

Today, in these times of cultural erosion, libraries are threatened by economic cutbacks, staff shortages, and the revolutionary invasion of electronic publishing, which transforms whole books into shining silver disks, to be "read" on a computer screen. For this technology, a library is as obsolete for

above

ONE OF THE NEWEST PUBLIC LIBRARIES IN THE UNITED STATES, THIS SPLENDID BUILDING IN BEVERLY HILLS, CALIFORNIA, WAS DESIGNED BY CHARLES MOORE.

left

THE LONDON LIBRARY OFFERS BROWSING AND WORKING SPACE TO THE CITY'S READING PUBLIC.

below

THE GROLIER CLUB WAS FOUNDED IN 1884 IN NEW YORK TO
ENCOURAGE LITERARY STUDY AND THE ARTS OF THE BOOK. THE
GROLIER HAS MANY FINE RARE BOOKS AND BINDINGS AND HOLDS
EXHIBITS THAT ARE OPEN TO THE PUBLIC.

books as the hot-water bottle is for warming one's bed. Visionary author Jorge Luis Borges forsaw a nightmare future for the library in this thankless age: "The Library will endure," he wrote, "illuminated, solitary, infinite, perfectly motionless, equipped with precious volumes, useless, incorruptible, secret."

Charles E. Pierce, Jr., director of the J. Pierpont Morgan Library in New York, addresses the issue from the viewpoint of his institution which, as well as possessing some of the world's rarest books, also houses priceless drawings and personal, handwritten manuscripts. "On recent display in the East Room was all the material that Muriel Spark compiled as she was writing her novel, *Symposium*," he says. "It begins with a little notebook in her handwriting, then she proceeds to a typescript. In the novel there is a dinner party scene and the material on display even included the seating plan of the people at this dinner

party. There are galleys, revisions, the first edition. You see the process of the work from beginning to end. With the introduction of the word processor, we aren't going to have that available to us anymore. We are going to be losing the creative process where you see the writer's mind at work. That seems to be a great loss, and we can only hope there will be some compensation we have not yet perceived."

But the library is fighting back. Ask the leaders of the great libraries, and they agree with Dr. Brian Lang, head of the London Library. "If the book were invented today," he says, "it would be hailed as a miracle of technology. It doesn't need batteries, you can scan it quickly, carry it in your jeans. There is no intermediate technology except . . . glasses. It would

be a brave man who digitized eighteen million books and then burned them."

But there is something about a public library even more precious than simply the contents of a book. Whether holding fine collections of precious works of art and authorship for specialists, or simply offering information and pleasure for the everyday reader, the public library is a resource institution that conveys human knowledge from one generation to another without fear or favor. Prospero, in Shakespeare's *The Tempest*, called his library his dukedom. Our urban and rural public libraries are our dukedoms, where, like royal families, we roam and graze at will, while our subjects, arranged humbly on shelves, stand poised at a touch to reveal their treasures. &

THE LIBRARY OF CONGRESS OCCUPIES
THREE BUILDINGS ON CAPITOL HILL
WHERE "AMERICA'S MEMORY" IS
PRESERVED IN OVER 20 MILLION BOOKS
AND PAMPHLETS IN 470 LANGUAGES,
"FITTING FOR THE NATIONAL LIBRARY OF
A DYNAMIC MULTICULTURAL
DEMOCRACY." SHOWN HERE, THE
JEFFERSON BUILDING.

THE MAIN READING ROOM IN THE JEFFERSON BUILDING OF THE LIBRARY OF
CONGRESS IN WASHINGTON, D.C. AMERICA'S OLDEST CULTURAL INSTITUTION,
THE LIBRARY RESPONDS TO 1.5 MILLION REQUESTS AND IS VISITED BY MORE
THAT 700,000 RESEARCHERS EACH YEAR. THOMAS JEFFERSON'S PERSONAL
LIBRARY FORMED THE CORE OF THE NATION'S LEGISLATIVE LIBRARY IN 1800.

RESOURCE DIRECTORY

Rare-Book Dealers/Shops

"Books may become obsolete for some purposes. The *Whitakers Almanac* type of book will disappear quite soon, as that sort of information will be available on CD–ROM. But reading is an aspect of behavior in human beings that proceeds at its own pace. The stress of modern life is such that the banker may take refuge in collecting books on ornithology to get away from work; similarly, the computer scientist may buy books on old-fashioned machines. For this reason alone, book-collecting will never die out."

Nicolas Barker, bibliophile and book curator

This is only a general listing. Regional guides can be found with listings of secondhand and rare-book dealers in your area. For a wonderful directory, consult the Antiquarian Booksellers' Association of America at 50 Rockefeller Plaza, New York, NY 10020 (212) 757-9395. This listing of ABAA members is updated annually. Many dealers publish catalogs and will send them on request.

United States

Archaeologica
Archaeology/Anthropology
707 Carlston Avenue
Oakland, CA 94610
(415) 832-1405

Barry R. Levin Science Fiction & Fantasy Literature
Science fiction, fantasy and horror, first editions, manuscripts
726 Santa Monica Blvd.
Suite 201
Santa Monica, CA 90401
(310) 458-6111

Bernard M. Rosenthal, Inc.
Incunabula, manuscripts and early printed books, bibliography, paleography
P.O. Box 5279
Berkeley, CA 94705
(510) 549-2532 (By appt. only)

Dawson's Book Shop
American history, photography, books about books, printing history, Western Americana, mountaineering
535 No. Larchmont Blvd.
Los Angeles, CA 90004
(213) 469-2186

Edwin V. Glaser, Rare Books
Science and medicine, early printed books, technology, natural history
P.O. Box 1765
Sausalito, CA 94966
(415) 332-1194 (By appt. only)

Eric Chaim Kline, Bookseller
Judaica and Hebraica, German language and literature, Middle East, travel guides
1343 3rd Street Promenade
Santa Monica, CA 90401
(310) 395-4747

Flashback Books
Sixties rarities
906 Samuel Drive
Petaluma, CA 94952
(707) 762-4714

Heritage Bookshop & Bindery, Inc.
Rare books, first editions, fine bindings, press books, manuscripts
8540 Melrose Avenue
Los Angeles, CA 90069
(310) 659-3674

Kenneth Starosciak
Art reference, American art, architecture, antiques, textiles
117 Wilmot
San Francisco, CA 94115
(415) 346-0650 (By appt. only)

Serendipity Books Inc.
Modern first editions, English and American literature, screenplays, little magazines, appraisals
1201 University Avenue
Berkeley, CA 94702
(510) 841-7455

Pepper & Stern—Rare Books
Rare cinema material, detective fiction, autographs, and manuscripts
1980 Cliff Drive, Suite 224
Santa Barbara, CA 93109
(see additional listing under Massachusetts)
(805) 963-1025 (By appt. only)

Angler's & Shooter's Bookshelf
Angling, shooting, sporting art
Box 178
Goshen, CT 06756
(203) 491-2500 (By appt. only)

McBlain Books
Africa, African-American, Asia and Pacific, Central and Latin America, Middle East
2348 Whitney Avenue
P.O. Box 5062
Hamden, CT 06518
(203) 281-0400 (By appt. only)

Timothy Mawson Books
Fine gardening and other horticultural volumes
Main Street
New Preston, CT 06777
(203) 868-7886

Trebizond Rare Books
Travels, English, Continental and American literature, Americana
Main Street, P.O. Box 2430
New Preston, CT 06777
(203) 868-2621 (By appt. only)

previous page
Robert Louis Stevenson reading in bed.

Whitlock Farm Bookseller

Oldest and largest seller of rare and used books in Connecticut
20 Sperry Road
Bethany, CT 06524
(203) 393-1240

William Reese Co.

General rare books, Americana
409 Temple Street
New Haven, CT 06551
(203) 789-8081

Oak Knoll Books

Books about books, bibliography, history of printing, book arts
414 Delaware Street
New Castle, DE 19720
(302) 328-7232

Booked Up

1209 31st Street, NW
Washington, DC 20007
(202) 965-3244

William Hale Antiquarian Books

Art reference, music, travel, appraisals
1222 31st Street, NW
Washington, DC 20007
(202) 338-8272

Grove Antiquarian Books

Rare books from Florida and Coconut Grove authors, science fiction, and architecture
3318 Virginia Street
Coconut Grove, FL 33133
(305) 444-5362

Robert A. Hittel Bookseller

General rare books
Plaza 3000 Shopping Center
3020 Shopping Center
3020 N. Federal Highway
Fort Lauderdale, FL 33306
(305) 563-1752

Books & Books Antiquarian & Used Book Room

Main store
296 Aragon Avenue
Coral Gables, FL 33134
(305) 442-4408

also at 933 Lincoln Road
Miami Beach, FL 33134
(305) 532-3222

Stonehill's Books

2606 Nottingham Court So.
Champaign, IL 61821
(217) 359-5289

Quill & Brush

Modern first editions, American and English literature, signed and inscribed books
P.O. Box 5365
Rockville, MD 20848
(301) 460-3700 (By appt. only)

Ars Libri, Ltd.

Art, art reference, and illustrated books
560 Harrison Avenue
Boston, MA 02118
(617) 357-5212

Bromer Booksellers

Rare books, literary first editions, fine bindings, miniature and illustrated books
607 Boylston Street
Boston, MA 02116
(617) 247-2828

Edward J. Lefkowicz, Inc.

Books on the sea, naval, maritime, whaling, polar and Pacific voyages
43 Fort Street
P.O. Box 630
Fairhaven, MA 02719
(508) 997-6839
(By mail or appt.)

J & J Lubrano

Musical autographs and manuscripts, rare printed music, musical literature and dance books
39 Hollenbeck Avenue
Great Barrington, MA 01230
(413) 528-5799 (By appt. only)

Ken Lopez Bookseller

General, modern first editions
51 Huntington Road
Hadley, MA 01035
(413) 584-4827

Pepper & Stern—Rare Books

Rare cinema material, detective fiction, autographs, and manuscripts
355 Boylston Street
Boston, MA 02116
(617) 421-1880

Peter L. Masi

General rare books and first editions from the 19th and 20th centuries
P.O. Box B
17 Central Street
Montague, MA 01351
(413) 367-2628

Priscilla Juvelis, Inc.

Illustrated books, first editions, livres d'artiste, fine printing
150 Huntington Avenue
Suite SD-L
Boston, MA 02115
(617) 424-1895 (By appt. only)

The Book House

Children's books
9719 Manchester Road
Rockhill, MO 63119
(314) 968-4491

Glenn Books

American history, American and English literature, book arts, private press, bindings
323 East 55th Street
Kansas City, MO 64113
(816) 444-4447 (By appt. only)

Antic Hay Books

First-edition fiction, poetry, and drama
1405 Chestnut Avenue
Asbury Park, NJ 07712
(908) 774-4590 (By appt. only)

The Argosy Book Store carries a broad range of out-of-print books, modern first editions, maps, prints, art, Americana, medical, and autographs. Three sisters are co-owners of this rare repository of books, in business since the twenties.

**Between the Covers
Rare Books**
132 Kings Highway East
Haddonfield, NJ 08033
(609) 354-7665

D & D Galleries
*Bindings, sets, Lewis Carroll,
English and American literature*
P.O. Box 8413
Somerville, NJ 08876
(908) 874-3162 (By appt. only)

Joseph J. Felcone, Inc.
*American history, early
Americana, New Jersey,
general rare books from the
16th to 20th century*
P.O. Box 366
Princeton, NJ 08540
(609) 924-0539 (By appt. only)

Acanthus Books
Decorative arts
48 West 22nd Street
New York, NY 10010
(212) 463-0750

Aleph-Bet Books, Inc.
*Children's books, fairy tales,
and myths*
218 Waters Edge
Valley Cottage, NY 10989
(914) 268-7410 (By appt. only)

Archivia
Decorative arts
944 Madison Avenue
New York, NY 10021
(212) 439-9194

Argosy Book Store, Inc.
*First editions, art, Americana,
medical, maps and prints,
autographs*
116 East 59th Street
New York, NY 10022
(212) 753-4455

Bauman Rare Books
*General rare books from 16th
to 20th centuries*
1215 Locust Street
Philadelphia, PA 19107
(215) 546-6473

also at the Waldorf-Astoria
301 Park Avenue
New York, NY 10022
(212) 759-8300

Books of Wonder
Children's books
132 Seventh Avenue
New York, NY 10011
(212) 989-3271

E.K. Schreiber
*Incunabula, early printed books,
humanism and Renaissance,
early illustrated books*
285 Central Park West
New York, NY 10024
(212) 873-3180 (By appt. only)

F.A. Bernett, Inc.
*Art, architecture, archaeology,
illustrated books*
2001 Palmer Avenue
Larchmont, NY 10538
(914) 834-3026

**Gotham Book Mart
& Gallery, Inc.**
*Literary archives, letters and
manuscripts, modern first
editions, appraisals*
41 West 47th Street
New York, NY 10036
(212) 719-4448

High Ridge Books, Inc.
*Maps, color-plate books,
Americana, New York City*
P.O. Box 286
Rye, NY 10580
(914) 967-3332 (By appt. only)

H.P. Kraus
*Incunabula, illuminated and
text manuscripts, early science,
Americana and printed books*
16 East 46th Street
New York, NY 10017
(212) 687-4808

J and P Klemperer
400 Second Avenue
New York, NY 10010
(212) 684-5970

J.N. Bartfield
*Bindings, rare books, leather-
bound sets and singles,
color-plate books*
30 West 57th Street
New York, NY 10019
(212) 245-8890

Jonathan A. Hill, Bookseller, Inc.
*Science and medicine, natural
history, fine printing, early
printed books*
325 West End Avenue
New York, NY 10023-8143
(212) 496-7856 (By appt. only)

Judith L. Bowman—Books
*Fishing and hunting, allied
natural history, sporting
bibliographies*
Pound Ridge Road
Bedford, NY 10506
(914) 234-7543 (By appt. only)

L.W. Currey, Inc.
*Science fiction, 19th-century
American literature, modern
first editions*
Water Street (Box 187)
Elizabethtown, NY 12932
(518) 873-6477 (By appt. only)

The Mysterious Book Shop
*Crime fiction, reading and first
editions, autographed modern
editions, reference*
129 West 56th Street
New York, NY 10019
(212) 765-0900

New York Bound Bookshop
*Specializes in books documenting
all things New York*
50 Rockefeller Plaza
New York, NY 10020
(212) 245-8503

**Paulette Rose, Fine & Rare
Books**
*Literary women, feminism,
English, French literature*
360 East 72nd Street
New York, NY 10021
(212) 861-5607 (By appt. only)

The Private Library
*Kurt Thometz, library specialist
and organizer*
85 St. Marks Avenue
Brooklyn, NY
(718) 789-8764

Founded 75 years ago by Frances Steloff, the Gotham Book Mart is identified with many celebrated writers and artists. Tennessee Williams once clerked here, Gertrude Stein frequently dropped by, and Steloff built Gotham's legendary reputation by daring to carry books by "fringe" authors James Joyce, Henry Miller, and D. H. Lawrence. Gotham still carries small-press books, poetry, American and English classics, and is a hub for literary events.

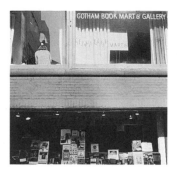

Strand Book Store, Inc.
General rare books, first editions, art and photography, books about books, Americana, appraisals
828 Broadway at 12th Street
New York, NY 10003
(212) 473-1452

Stubbs Books & Prints
153 East 70th Street
New York, NY 10021
(212) 772-3120

Timothy Trace Bookseller
Art reference, crafts and trades, textiles and fashion
144 Red Mill Road
Cortlandt Manor, NY 10566
(914) 528-4074 (By appt. only)

Ursus Books
Fine art books and prints
981 Madison Avenue
New York, NY 10021
(212) 772-8787

Wurlitzer-Bruck
Music, books on music, musical autographs, and ephemera
60 Riverside Drive
New York, NY 10024
(212) 787-6431 (By appt. only)

Chapel Hill Rare Books
Modern first editions, 19th- and 20th-century British and American literature, rare Americana, exploration and travel, quality books in all fields
P.O. Box 456
Carrboro, NC 27510
(919) 929-8351 (By appt. only)

David J. Holmes, Autographs
Autographs, 19th-century first editions, presentation copies, original drawings
230 So. Broad Street
Philadelphia, PA 19102
(215) 735-1083

F. Thomas Heller
Early science and medicine, early psychiatry and psychoanalysis
P.O. Box 356
Swarthmore, PA 19081
(215) 543-3582 (By appt. only)

George S. MacManus Company
American history, rare Americana, American military history, American and English first editions
1317 Irving Street
Philadelphia, PA 19107
(215) 735-4456

Rulon-Miller Books
Books, maps, prints and manuscripts from the British and American Virgin Islands, Caribbean, and Central America
P.O. Box 46
Bristol, RI 02809
(401) 253-7824 (June–Sept.)
also in Virgin Islands
Red Hook
Box 41
St. Thomas, VI 00802
(809) 775-6308 (Oct.–May)

Jo Ann Reisler, Ltd.
Children's books, illustrated books, early paper dolls and paper toys
360 Glyndon Street N.E.
Vienna, VA 22180
(703) 938-2967 (By appt. only)

England

There are over 24 bookstores in Hay-on-Wye, Wales, all specializing, all wonderful. It would be impossible to list them all. The two biggest are:

Booth Books
Over 400,000 volumes
Hay Castle & Lion Street
Hay-on-Wye
Hereford HR3 5AA
(0497) 820322

Hay Cinema Bookshop
The Old Cinema
Castle Street
Hay-on-Wye
Hereford HR3 5DF
(0497) 820071

Jarndyce
19th-century English literature, economics, political and social histories
46 Gt. Russell Street
London WC1
(0171) 631-4220

Robert Connelly
History of medicine and science
The Bookshop
31/35 Gt. Ormond Street
London WCIN 3HZ
(0171) 430-1349

Travis & Emery
17 Cecil Court
London WC2N 4EZ
(0171) 240-2129

Watkins Books Ltd.
Mysticism, astrology, occult
19-21 Cecil Court
London WC2N 4EZ
(0171) 836-2182

Henry Sotheran Ltd.
English literature, natural history, architecture
2-5 Sackville Street
London W1X 2DP
(0171) 439-6151

Bernard J. Shapero Rare Books
Voyages and travel, natural history, English literature, art, architecture, modern first editions
80 Holland Park Avenue
London W11 3RE
(0171) 493-0876

Russell Rare Books
Natural history, travel, architecture, English literature
Grays Antique Market
58 Davies Street
London W1Y 1LB
(0171) 629-0532
(0171) 491-8599

Bernard Quaritch Ltd.
Incunabula, early printed; English literature, bibliography, Orientalia, politics, philosophy, economics
5-8 Lower John Street
London W1R 4AU
(0171) 734-2983

Maggs Brothers Ltd.
Rare books, illuminated manuscripts, autographed letters
50 Berkeley Square
London W1X 6EL
(0171) 493-7160

Gloucester Road Bookshop
Large stock of Graham Greene first editions and related material
123 Gloucester Road
London SW7 4TE
(0171) 370-3503

Book Fairs

We're great book buyers—Hugh and I go to tag sales, auctions, wherever we can discover books that are worth finding, though they may not have first-edition quality. We recently found a William Shirer first edition of *Berlin Diaries*, which had been out of print, and gave it to my son, who is interested in history. We found *Sporting Tour*, the two-volume book published in 1925 which is on my end table in the living room, at a country auction or an estate sale. I'm planning on giving it to friends who are interested in the subject. The books I pile up on my end tables in the living room are the ones I plan to do something about — to give as gifts or give away."

Tiziana Hardy, architect

This is a partial list of general interest book fairs that are open to the public. The Library of Congress's Fanfare for Words *by Bernadine Clark includes a more comprehensive directory of book fairs and festivals around the United States with contact information. Another excellent source is* A. B. Bookman Weekly, *P.O. Box AB, Clifton, NJ 07015; (201) 772-0020. Check your local newspapers for fairs and festivals coming to your area.*

**Antiquarian Booksellers'
Association of America**
50 Rockefeller Plaza
New York, NY 10020
(212) 757-9395

The ABAA holds four or five book fairs a year to sell books and educate the public about book collecting and fine books. Their New York–based fair is the oldest in the country and features collectors' items from around 125 book dealers from the U.S. and Europe. The following is a list of other ABAA book fair locations and usual dates.

San Francisco/Los Angeles
Time of year: February (held in each city on an alternating basis)

New York City
Time of year: mid to late April

Washington, DC
Time of year: September

Boston
Time of year: November

Chicago
Time of year: May (held only during odd years)

Greater St. Louis Book Fair
8433 Mid County
Industrial Court
Vinita Park, MO 63114
(314) 533-0671
Time of year: April

The Greater St. Louis Book Fair is a five-day book sale featuring over a million books, magazines, and records, most priced at $5 or less. Open to the general public, finds can include first editions to classic children's books.

Vassar Book Sale
Vassar Club of Washington
2737 Devonshire Place NW
Washington, DC 20008
(202) 667-1592
Time of year: May

The Vassar Book Sale, a legendary used-book sale, draws book dealers from around the country and regularly features an estimated 100,000 volumes in nearly seventy categories from general interest to rare books. Money raised goes toward Vassar scholarships for Washington-area students.

**Chicago Printers Row
Book Fair**
1727 S. Indiana #104
Chicago, IL 60616
(312) 987-1980
Time of year: June

This Midwest book festival happens indoors and outdoors in downtown Chicago's historic Printers Row district. Street entertainment includes live music, stories for all ages, and a troupe of street performers. Exhibits of old, new, rare, and used books by more than 100 booksellers and publishers in the United States and Canada combine with author readings, book signings, and book-as-art demonstrations for a literary Father's Day weekend.

New York Is Book Country
Time of year: September
This six-hour Sunday street fair is the largest one-day book event in the United States. Fifth Avenue is closed down between 48th and 57th Streets and pedestrians and booklovers are free to wander and survey books from over 165 exhibitors. Literary games and contests along with thousands of books fill Antiquarian Row and the half-mile main book thoroughfare. An open-air stage features readings, mixed-media performances, and an auction of book-related items and services. Three book-and-author events supply sit-down nourishment in downtown Manhattan. This fair is part of a three-day literary weekend that features over 85 events in all five boroughs.

Library of Congress
USA 20c

Small Press Book Fair

20 West 44th Street
New York, NY 10036
(212) 764-7021
Time of year: mid-September

Set in a landmark building
of the General Society of
Mechanics and Tradesmen, this
two-day event features writers
and writing from national and
international small and independent publishers. More than 100
exhibitors sell literary and popular works, ranging from fine
letterpress books to cooking
and travel books not readily
available in bookstores.

Trinity Antiquarian Book Fair

400 Second Avenue
New York, NY 10010
(212) 684-5970
Time of year: October

The Trinity Antiquarian Book
Fair, founded and run by Judy
and Peter Klemperer for the
past fifteen years, is held on the
fourth weekend in October on
the Upper West Side of
Manhattan. It draws an estimated 110 booksellers from
around the country and an
equally diverse group of
shoppers and perusers.

Kentucky Book Fair

P.O. Box 715
Frankfort, KY 40602
(502) 875-7000
Time of year: November

Staged in Frankfort on the
Saturday before Thanksgiving,
the Kentucky Book Fair takes a
classic approach to celebrating
books and reading. Between
eighty and ninety well-known
authors come with pens in hand
to autograph their books —
some 20,000 books are available at a 20 percent discount.
Work includes poetry, biography, fantasy, history, humor,
and art.

The Buckeye Book Fair

212 East Liberty Street
Wooster, OH 44691
(216) 264-1125
Time of year: November

A seven-hour book bazaar,
modeled on the Kentucky Book
Fair, the Buckeye Book Fair fills
Wooster's Fisher Auditorium
with readers, writers, and books
sold at a discount off the cover
price. More than eighty-five
writers from around the country,
as well as local talents, participate.

Miami Book Fair International

300 Northeast Second Avenue
Room 1501
Miami, FL 33132
(305) 237-3258
Time of year: November

The largest book fair in the
United States, this Miami-based
extravaganza transforms the
downtown campus of Miami-

**The Library of Congress established the Center for the Book
in 1977 to stimulate public interest in books, reading, and
libraries. To mark the Center's national reading campaign in
1984, Bradbury Thompson was commissioned to design
commemorative stamps, "A nation of readers."**

above left

**The Jefferson Building of the Library of Congress illustrated
on stamp.**

below

**An adaptation of a Mathew Brady daguerreotype of Abraham
Lincoln reading to his son, Tad.**

A Nation of
Readers
USA 20c

Dade Community College into
a booklover's dream. It features
books from more than 300
booksellers from around the
country and includes a variety
of pre-fair events which salute
books and reading with a cele-
bratory blend of literary and
performance art. Over 250
authors from around the world
participate. Open to the public.

Center for Book Arts Annual Open House

626 Broadway
New York, NY 10012
(212) 460-9768
Time of year: December

The Annual Open House is an
opportunity for book artists to
sell their handcrafted books and
educate the public about book
arts. Letterpress, hand-bound
books, one-of-a-kind artists'
books, literature, handmade
cookbooks, and limited edition
titles are featured. Open to
the public.

Bookbinders/Restorers

"Paper remembers everything that happens to it. Paper remembers it all. So the first thing you do, when you sit down to work, is figure out how you're going to trick that piece of paper. You've got to trick it into letting you work in ways that won't change it, forever . . . the work may not ever be perfect, because perfect is forgery. Everything you do must have your name on it. Every repair you make must stand out clearly as a repair. You know what perfection is, but you do not allow yourself to achieve it."

From What a Man Weighs *by Sherry Kramer (Broadway Play Publishing, Inc.)*

Check the Yellow Pages for specialists or contact the American Institute for the Conservation of Historic and Artistic Works at 1717 K Street, NW, Suite 301, Washington, DC 20006, (202) 452-9545.

Yale University Conservation Division
P.O. Box 208240
Yale Station
New Haven, CT 06520
(203) 432-1711

Denis Gouey Bookbinding Studio
Hand binding; sells eclectic mix of first editions and other finds
P.O. Box 383
Norfolk, CT 06058
(203) 542-5063

Society of American Archivists
600 South Federal Street
Suite 504
Chicago, IL 60605
(312) 922-0140

Claudia Cohen
Hand binding; limited editions
One Cottage Street
Easthampton, MA 01027
(413) 527-6007

Wide Awake Garage
P.O. Box 449
Easthampton, MA 01027
(413) 527-8044

Jerilyn Glenn Davis
1140 Broadway
Room #1001
New York, NY 10001
(212) 889-2239

Guild of Book Workers
Produces a handbook of binders, conservators, printers, and paper makers
521 Fifth Avenue
New York, NY 10175
(212) 757-6454

Park Slope Bookbindery
General hand binding; specializes in binding musical scores
Francois V. Scott
11 Park Place
Brooklyn, NY 11217
(718) 857-0727

Conservation Laboratory
New York Public Library
42nd Street & Fifth Avenue
New York, NY 10018
(212) 930-0549

Paper Star Associates, Inc.
Book and paper conservation, fine binding
Nelly Balloffet
543 Illington Road
Ossining, NY 10562
(914) 941-8166

Eudaldo Ginesta
264 West 40th Street
8th Floor
New York, NY 10018
(212) 302-0303

Weitz Weitz & Coleman
1377 Lexington Avenue
New York, NY 10128
(212) 831-2213

Carolyn Chadwick
Refurbishes private libraries
789 West End Avenue
New York, NY 10025
(212) 865-5157

Angela Scott
Custom book binding; restoration
596 Broadway
Suite 902B
New York, NY 10012
(212) 431-5148

Judy Ivory
25 East 4th Street
New York, NY 10003
(212) 677-1015

Twelfth Night West
17 Enebro Road
Santa Fe, NM 87505
(505) 466-9015

Bridwell Conservation Laboratory
Southern Methodist University
Dallas, TX 75275
(214) 768-3733

England

U.K. Institute for Conservation
6 Whitehorse Mews
Westminster Bridge Road
London W14 8AJ

Bardel Bookbinding Ltd.
Hand binding and gold blocking
Unit D2, Alladin Workspace
426 Long Drive
Greenford UB6

Wyvern Bindery
Leather binding, limited editions, portfolios, restoration, and repair
Unit 052, 31 Clerkenwell Close
London ECI

Marba Bookbinding
63 Jeddo Road
London W12

Fairfax Bookbinders Ltd.
101 Farm Lane
London SW6

Alfred Maltby & Son Ltd.
28 & 30 St. Michaels Street
Oxford OX1 2EB

F. Sangorski & G. Sutcliffe Ltd.
175r Bermondsey Street
London SE1

Bell Books Ltd.
16 Junction Road
Ealing
London N7 8LJ

Library Furnishings

I pile up books on the bottom of a carrel that I designed, keeping my writing notes and material on the shelves below so everything I need for the project I'm working on is all in one place. When I'm done, I just wheel the carrel back over to the book wall and reshelve the books. When I read for pleasure, I enjoy reading in bed and pile up pillows against its soft headrest. Pillows are the best, unheralded reading prop."

Diana Balmori, landscape architect

This is a partial list. A good illustrated source is Sunset's "Ideas for Great Wall Systems." Many museums and art houses publish catalogs that include library furniture.

Cramer Inc.
Seating and utility products; catalog available
625 Adams Street
Kansas City, KS 66105
(913) 621-6700

Baker Furniture Co.
1661 Monroe N.W.
Grand Rapids, MI 49505
(616) 361-7321

Henredon Furniture Industries
P.O. Box 70
Morganton, NC 28680-0070
(404) 886-1476

Lineage Home Furnishings, Inc.
P.O. Box 11188
High Point, NC 27265
(910) 454-6688

Ethan Allen Inc.
Ethan Allen Drive
P.O. Box 1966
Danbury, CT 06813-1966
(203) 743-8000

Scandinavian Gallery
Wood and plastic units
30 Lincoln Plaza
New York, NY 10023

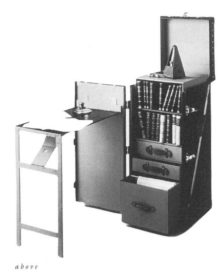

above

Louis Vuitton's book trunk and secretaire, designed for Leopold Stokowski in 1936, is available in finely crafted reproductions.

Wall Furniture Outlet
Stores throughout New York and New Jersey.
(800) 345-6936

Staples Office Supplies
Utility furniture
Stores located in several states including Kentucky, Florida, Delaware, New York, Ohio, Virginia, and several New England states. Catalog and delivery available.
(800) 333-3330

Photographer: Robert Lautman

left

A revolving bookstand at Thomas Jefferson's home in Monticello. Believed to be designed by Jefferson and made at the Monticello joinery, the bookstand folds into a cube when not in use and adjoins a favorite reading chair. In the background, Jefferson's unique bookcases can quickly be transformed into traveling book boxes.

Roche-Bobois USA Ltd.
183 Madison Avenue
New York, NY 10016
(212) 889-5304

Putnam Rolling Ladder Co., Inc.
32 Howard Street
New York, NY 10013
(212) 226-5147

Levenger
*Catalog totally devoted to library
furniture and accessories*
P.O. Box 1256
Delray Beach, FL 33447
(800) 545-0242

Eximious of London
*Catalog of library furniture
and accessories imported from
England, France, and Italy*
201 Northfield Road
Northfield, IL 60093-3372
(800) 221-9464

Louis Vuitton
*Library travel furniture
by catalog*
130 East 59th Street
New York, NY 10022
(212) 572-9700

Sentimento
306 East 61st Street
New York, NY 10021
(212) 750-3111

Art & Artifact
*Library furniture and accessories
by catalog*
2451 Enterprise East Parkway
Twinsburg, OH 44087
(800) 231-6766

Howell Design, Inc.
Reader's window
192 Thomas Lane
Stowe, VT 05672
(800) 867-7869

England

Balmforth Engineering Ltd.
Shelving and furniture systems
Library Systems Division
Dallow Road
Luton, Beds LU1 1TE

Simplex
Wooden shelving and bookcases
High Street
Oldland Common
Bristol BS15 6TA

Utilitarian Folding Bookcases
*Folding bookcases in beech;
natural, white, mahogany*
4 Wren Wood
Welwyn Garden City
Herts AL7 1QG

Christopher Gibbs Ltd.
Antique library furniture
8 Vigo Street
London W1Z 1AL

Westenholz Antiques Ltd.
Antique library furniture
68 Pimlico Road
London SW1W 8LS

Bookcases/Cabinets:
Manufactured
Stock, Custom, and
Semicustom

Aristokraft, Inc.
P.O. Box 420
Jasper, IN 47546
(812) 482-2527

above, left to right

A "scooter stool" that supports up to 300 pounds, a rolling "stop-step" ladder with wheels that lock in place, and the original rolling step stool, "kik-step"—all available at Cramer, Inc.

Starmark Cabinets
P.O. Box 84810
Sioux Falls, SD 57118
(605) 335-8600

Rutt Custom Cabinetry
P.O. Box 129
Goodville, PA 17528
(717) 445-6751

KraftMaid Cabinetry, Inc.
16052 Industrial Parkway
Middlefield, OH 44062
(216) 632-5333

Haas Cabinet Co. Inc.
625 W. Utica Street
Sellersburg, IN 47172
(800) 457-6458

Bookcases/Cabinets:
Modular Systems,
Ready–to–Assemble

eurodesign, ltd.
359 State Street
Los Altos, CA 94022
(415) 941-7761

Ikea Area East
Plymouth Commons
496 West Germantown Pike
Plymouth Meeting, PA 19462
(610) 834-0180

*Stores located in New York,
New Jersey, Washington, DC,
Baltimore, Philadelphia,
Pittsburgh, and Houston*

Planum, Inc.
8920 Beverly Boulevard
Los Angeles, CA 90048
(310) 288-0070

Techline
500 South Division Street
Waunakee, WI 53597
(800) 356-8400

Allmilmo Corporation
70 Clinton Road
Fairfield, NJ 07004
(201) 227-2502

Steel Shelving

**A & D Steel Equipment
Company**
11-35 31st Drive
Long Island City, NY 11106
(718) 728-4100

**Able Steel Equipment
Company**
50-02 23rd Street
Long Island City, NY 11101
(718) 361-9240

**Adjustable Steel Products
Company**
276 Fifth Avenue
Suite 906
New York, NY 10016
(212) 686-1030

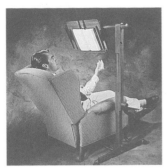

Shelving

Shelf Shop
1295 1st Avenue
New York, NY 10021
(212) 988-7246

A Building Block
314 11th Avenue
New York, NY 10001
(212) 714-9333

Lee/Rowan Company
900 S. Highway Drive
Fenton, MO 63026
(800) 325 6150

Superior Wood Shelving
107 S. Cashiers East
P.O. Box 1475
Cashiers, NC 28717
(704) 743-9040

Hippodrome Hardware Inc.
23 West 45th Street
New York, NY 10036
(212) 840-2791

SICO Room Makers
P.O. Box 1169
Minneapolis, MN 55440
(800) 328-6138

Moldings and Millwork

**Focal Point
Architectural Products**
P.O. Box 93327
Atlanta, GA 30377
(800) 662-5550

Ornamental Compositions
248 West 88th Street
New York, NY 10024
(212) 799-6337

Wood Moulding & Millwork
Producers Association
1730 S.W. Skyline Blvd.
Portland, OR 97221
(503) 292-9288

Creative Additions, Ltd.
134 West 26th Street
New York, NY 10010
(212) 679-1515

Silverton Victorian Millworks
P.O. Box 2987
Durango, CO 81302
(800) 933-3930

Fypon Molded Millwork
22 West Pennsylvania Avenue
Stewartstown, PA 17363
(800) 537-5349

Trompe l'Oeil Fabrics, Wallpapers

Blumenthal
42-20 Twelfth Street
Long Island City, NY 11101
(718) 361-1234

Brunschwig & Fils
979 Third Avenue
New York, NY 10022
(212) 838-7878

Clarence House Fabrics Ltd.
211 East 58th Street
New York, NY 10022
(212) 752-2890

boussac of france, inc.
979 Third Avenue
New York, NY 10022
(212) 421-0534

above

The Barrister Bookcases produced for Levenger by Hale Manufacturing Company revives a design of the past. The center section holds books up to 10 inches high, with upper and lower sections holding books up to 12 inches. Each section is 9½ inches deep and 32 inches wide. Available through catalog in natural and dark cherry, medium oak, and walnut.

top left

Eximious of London's mahogany faux bookshelf cabinet is designed for the bibliophile who enjoys entertaining in the library.

top right

Reader's Window, by Howell Design, eliminates reading discomfort from neck and upper back fatigue. This ergonometric bookstand positions books at or above eye level and can be adjusted to accommodate reading in chairs, beds, or on the floor.

Library Lighting

A lighting fixture is not a passive object but an active maker of place. There is no single solution as there is no single definition of personal. When your lamp is on, it should fill you with a need to read and reward you with its respectful silent light."

Peter Barna

This is a partial list. Consult the Yellow Pages for additional companies in your area.

Nesson Lamps Inc.
420 Railroad Way
Mamaroneck, NY 10543
(914) 698-7799

Cedric Hartman, Inc.
1116-18 Jackson Street
Box 3842
Omaha, NE 68103-0842
(402) 344-4474

Mirak Inc.
1049 Third Avenue
New York, NY 10021

George Kovacs Lighting, Inc.
IDCNY Center 2
30-20 Thompson Avenue
Long Island City, NY 11101
(718) 392-8190

Artemide, Inc.
1980 New Highway
Farmingdale, NY 11735
(516) 694-9292

Flos Incorporated
200 McKay Road
Huntington Station, NY 11746
(516) 549-2745

LUXO Lamp Corporation
36 Midland Avenue
P.O. Box 951
Port Chester, NY 10573
(914) 937-4433

**ZELCO Industries Inc.
(LUXO Italiana Spa)**
630 South Columbus Avenue
Mount Vernon, NY 10550
(914) 699-6230

BOYD Lighting Company
56 Twelfth Street
San Francisco, CA 94103-1293
(415) 431-4300

Rejuvenation Lamp & Fixture Company
1100 South East Avenue
Portland, OR 97214
(503) 231-1900

Capri Lighting
6430 E. Slauson Avenue
Los Angeles, CA 90040
(213) 726-1800

Cooper Lighting
400 Busse Road
Elk Grove Village, IL 60007
(800) 323-8705

CSL Lighting Manufacturing
27615 Avenue Hopkins
Valencia, CA 91355
(805) 257-4155

Juno Lighting, Inc.
2001 S. Mt. Prospect Road
Des Plaines, IL 60017
(800) 367-5866

Lightolier/Genlyte
100 Lighting Way
Secaucus, NJ 07096
(800) 628-8692

Translite Systems
1300 Industrial Road
Suite 22
San Carlos, CA 94070
(800) 473-3242

Lighting Research Center
*Information and publications
of interest*
Rensselaer Polytechnic Institute
Troy, NY 12180-3590
(518) 276-8716

**The Illuminating Engineering
Society of North America**
120 Wall Street
New York, NY 10005-4001
(212) 248-5000

American Lighting Association
435 North Michigan Avenue
Chicago, IL 60611
(800) 274-4484

THE TEN BEST READING LIGHTS

Usability, flexibility, and aesthetic design were the criteria by which lighting specialist Peter Barna chose light fixtures for book people. Three of them are in the Museum of Modern Art's esteemed Design Collection. Many of these models come in floor, table, and wall versions and are designed to accommodate user needs and furniture placement.

1

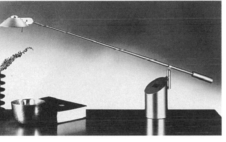

2

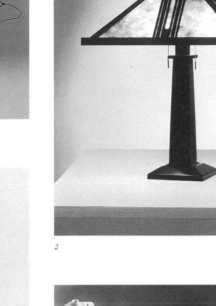

3

4

5 6 7 8

9

10

1

"Parentesi," a cable-hung floor-to-ceiling lamp, can be angled up for indirect light, turned to the wall to light a painting, and down for direct light. MOMA Design Collection. Manufacturer: Flos Inc.

2

The "Glasgow" table lamp, used extensively in public libraries, projects an arts and crafts aesthetic. Produced by Boyd Lighting Co. in hardwood with natural or black lacquer finish. 26 inches tall; 7-inch-diameter base.

3

Cedric Hartman floor lamp "1u WV" is an update on the classic V-shaped pharmacy lamp. MOMA Design.

4

Robert Sonneman's evocative "feather," an adjustable halogen lamp with arm rotating 360 degrees, comes in table, floor, and wall-mounted models. Manufactured by George Kovacs Lighting, Inc., NY.

5

"The Skyline" floor lamp from Rejuvenation Lamp & Fixture Company. Wired with four brass pull-chains for each 60 watt bulb, it delivers maximum light. 69 inches tall; 12-inch-square base. Variety of glass shades and metal finishes.

6

Lorenzo Porcelli's "Corona" floor lamp. Light filtered through rice-paper shade creates subdued illumination. Manufactured by Luxo Italiana Spa; distributed by Zelco Industries. MOMA Design Collection.

7

Enzo Mari's "aggregato stelo" floor lamp for Artemide with sliding slides on a fixed shaft, 11¾ by 63¼ inches high.

8

Mirak's classic "Olympe" table lamp can adjust height from 22 inches to 26.

9

Luxo's versatile halogen "task lighting system" with 40- or 25-inch swing arm is practical for desk, floor, and wall illumination.

10

One of the "Agusti Series" by Nessen Lamps features an adjustable 25-inch swing arm lamp. The series' wall, table, and floor lamps come in a wide range of heights, styles, and materials.

Library Accessories and Ephemera

B ooks may make a room, but by themselves don't make a true bibliophile. Telltale signs can be found all around a serious library. It is the book stands and library steps, magnifying glasses and bookmarks, slipcases and catalogs that distinguish shelves of books from a living library."

Martin Filler

above

Reproduction of the rare magnifying glass used by bibliophile Otto Bettman. Available from the Levenger catalog.

This is a partial list. Many museums, fine stores, and auction houses publish catalogs in which library accessories are included.

American Society of Bookplate Collectors and Designers
605 North Stoneman #F
Alhambra, CA 91801

Library of Congress
Card and Gift Shop and
Catalog
Information Office, Box A
Washington, DC 20540
(202) 287-5112

Starrhill Press
Booklovers' ephemera/catalog
P.O. Box 32342
Washington, DC 20007
(202) 686-6703

University Products, Inc.
517 Main Street
Holyoke, MA 01041
(413) 532-3372

DHPD
Bookmarks
405 Adams Street
Bedford Hills, NY 10507
(800) 648-5455

Ex Libris
Customized bookplates
521 Fifth Avenue
Suite 1700
New York, NY 10175
(800) 637-8728

The Library Shop
Book products and accessories
New York Public Library
42nd Street and Fifth Avenue
New York, NY 10018-2788
(212) 930-0641

Margo Mulholland
Bookplate Collector
250 West 22nd Street
New York, NY 10011

TALAS Division of Technical Library
568 Broadway
New York, NY 10012
(212) 219-0776

Light Impressions Corp.
439 Monroe Avenue
Rochester, NY 14607
(716) 271-8960

Conservation Materials, Ltd.
1395 Greg Street
Suite 110
Sparks, NV 89431
(702) 331-0582

The Library Friends' Shop
Public Library of Cincinnati
and Hamilton County
800 Vine Street
Library Square
Cincinnati, OH 45202-2071
(513) 369-6920

Diane Maurer Marbleized Papers
Marbleizing supplies and papers, books on the craft, and workshops offered
P.O. Box 78
Spring Mills, PA 16875
(814) 422-8651

Brodart
1609 Memorial Avenue
Williamsport, PA 17705
(800) 233-8959

Monticello
Catalog of reproductions of Monticello accessories
Thomas Jefferson
Memorial Foundation, Inc.
Monticello Catalog
P.O. Box 318
Charlottesville, VA 22902
(800) 243-1743

Demco
Box 7488
Madison, WI 53707
(608) 241-1201

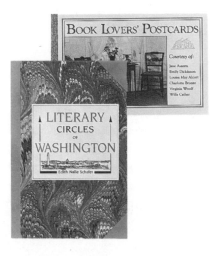

top

Commissioned by the Cincinnati Public Library from David Howell & Company, this 14-karat gold-plated bookmark was inspired by Michael Frasca's book fountain sculpture.

above right

Literary guidebooks and "Book Lovers" postcards are just two of the many book-related accessories and ephemera that have made Starrhill Press, a division of Elliot & Clark Publishing, popular among bibliophiles.

Great Libraries of the World

Austria
Melk
Baroque Library

Vienna
Austrian National Library

Belgium
Brussels
Royal Library

Czech Republic
Prague
Strahov Monastery

England
Cambridge
Pepys Library
(Magdalene College)

London
British Museum

Manchester
John Rylands Library

Oxford
Bodleian Library

France
Chantilly
Bibliothèque Spoelberch de
Lovenjoul

Paris
Bibliothèque d'Arsenal
Bibliothèque Nationale

Germany
Munich
Bavarian State Library

Greece
Patmos
Monastery of St. John

Ireland
Dublin
Trinity College

Italy
Florence
Biblioteca Mediceo-
Laurenziana

Milan
Biblioteca Ambrosiana

Modena
The Duke's Library

Rome
The Vatican Library

Martinique
Fort-de-France
Bibliothèque Schoelcher

Russia
Moscow
Russian State Library

St. Petersburg
Russian National Library

Spain
El Escorial
Library of the Royal Monastery

Madrid
Palace Library

Seville
Biblioteca Colombina

United States
Austin, TX
University Library

Cambridge, MA
Harvard University Library

New Haven, CT
Yale University Library

New York, NY
New York Public Library
Pierpont Morgan Library

Princeton, NJ
Princeton University Library

San Marino, CA
Henry E. Huntington Library

Washington, DC
Library of Congress

CREDITS

Endpapers, pages 94, 164: "Templiers," a wall fabric designed by Daniel Beugnon for boussac of france, inc. **ii, 56:** "Bibliothèque," wallpaper designed by Richard Neas; Brunschwig & Fils. **iv:** *The Bookworm,* a German genre painting by Carl Sqitzeg (1808–1878). Courtesy of Otto L. Bettman from his collection at the Bettman Archives, Inc., New York. **2:** "*Librairie P. Desbois*" courtesy of S. Emmerling, Antiquarian Bookseller & Print Dealer, Amsterdam. **4:** *The Bookseller* courtesy of S. Emmerling, Antiquarian Bookseller & Print Dealer, Amsterdam. **5:** "Teaching an Elephant to Read." Courtesy of Otto L. Bettman, from his book *The Delights of Reading* (published by David R. Godine in association with The Center for the Book at the Library of Congress). **92–93:** Photographs by Antoine Bootz. **125, 127:** Photographs of individual craft objects by Ihara. **126:** Photograph courtesy of Adelaide de Menil. **138:** Clarence House fabric, "Bibliothèque," designed by Kazumi Yoshida. **158–159:** Custom-designed bookplates collected by Margo Mulholland. **159:** Excerpts from "Artworks of Possession" by Jill Gerston. *Traditional Home.* November 1992. **195:** Excerpt from *Bibliomania* by Roger Rosenblatt. **196–201:** Information excerpts from *The Care of Fine Books* by Jane Greenfield (Lyons & Burford, Publishers). **196–198:** Dan Chatman pen-and-ink drawings. **206:** Wallcovering designed by Piero Fornasetti—Blumenthal, Inc. **231:** Photographs of New York Public Library, © Peter Aaron/Esto courtesy of New York Public Library and Erica Stoller. **232:** Photographs of Library of Congress by Michael Dersin. **233:** Robert Louis Stevenson reading in bed. Courtesy of Otto L. Bettman, from his book *The Delights of Reading.* **239:** Commemorative stamps courtesy of The Center for the Book at the Library of Congress. **240:** Excerpt from Sherry Kramer's play *What a Man Weighs* (Broadway Play Publishing, Inc.). **241 (bottom):** Jefferson bookstand photograph by Robert Lautman.

Index